HEARING IN TECHNICOLOR

HEARING IN TECHNICOLOR

MINDSET SHIFTS within a

MULTICULTURAL CONGREGATION

MARK HEARN

WITH DARCY WILEY

B&H
PUBLISHING
NASHVILLE, TENNESSEE

Published by B&H Publishing Group
Nashville, Tennessee

Dewey Decimal Classification: 261.8
Subject Heading: CHURCH / ETHNIC RELATIONS / CHURCH AND
RACE RELATIONS

May the next generation of the church lovingly embrace the beautiful diversity of our country and prove that spiritual unity is a mighty evangelistic force. Lovingly dedicated to my grandchildren:

Alex
Daniel
Tianya
William
Anna Kate
Layne
Andie
Lindy
Keri Jo
Darcy

Contents

Foreword

*H*earing *in Technicolor* is moving us in the right direction!
You don't have to look very far to realize that our communities are changing. The nations are literally being brought into our own backyards. The opportunity to fulfill the Great Commission is more tangible than it has ever been. This should excite Great Commission churches! Can you imagine having a church that reflects its surrounding community? Picture walking into church on a Sunday morning and seeing different ethnic groups, hearing the different languages, and it's all in your own church. As the world around us continues to change and diversify, it is imperative that our church leaders find a new way of doing ministry. The numbers of declining and dying churches in America are staggering, but it doesn't have to be that way!

Pastor Mark is succeeding in an area where many are struggling. First Baptist Duluth is reaching and leading a multicultural community. When I first met Mark, it was obvious that God's hand was on him. I don't know if you have ever met someone and thought, "Something is different about that person," but that is exactly what I thought about Mark. When I watched him from afar, he was charismatic, engaging, and treated each person with the same value and respect. His heart for all people was evident.

I continued to follow him from a distance and realized that God is using him to do something very special.

When you read this book, you will see a man whose biblical convictions and theological view are the driving force for all that he is doing. He is not trying to lead a trend or tokenize his church. The movement he is leading was birthed out of a God-conviction. As you read through this book, it will be easy to see that it is flooded with stories that have the fingerprints of God all over them.

Mark Hearn is a trailblazer in his ministry approach and perspective. He gets it! As you read *Hearing in Technicolor*, you will quickly and clearly see that Mark is doing something unique in his ministry context. The stories are saturated with God-moments, and his approach to a multicultural ministry is one that should be studied by many.

If you are living in a community that has rapid growth in diversification and want to know how to reach the community without losing your church, then this is the book for you. You will read about his journey of taking a declining monoethnic church to a growing multiethnic church.

Mark offers deep theological insights and translates them into everyday practical applications. He shows what it looks like not only to preach the Great Commission but, most important, to live it out. He has written this book in a way that informs, inspires, and ignites a passion to have a heart for the nations, just as Christ intended for us to have.

As a young pastor, I have found myself in a situation similar to the one Mark walked into, a congregation that was monoethnic and didn't match the city around it. Being someone who is currently leading a church that reflects my community, I can wholeheartedly support the mission, vision, and direction of this book. Whether you're pastoring a thriving church or a dying church, I believe this book can take your church to another level of gospel impact.

Hearing in Technicolor should be taught in seminaries across our country and used to prepare our future pastors and church planters to reach our world for Jesus. It's a must-read for any church leader.

Through this book, may God ignite a deep conviction and passion in you, equipping you to reach the nations in your backyard.

Dr. Noe Garcia, head pastor
North Phoenix Baptist Church

▼ ▼ ▼

Hearing in Technicolor

*During the night Paul had a vision in which a
Macedonian man was standing and pleading with him,
"Cross over to Macedonia and help us!" (Acts 16:9)*

*A vision without the ability to execute it is
called hallucinating! Every God-given vision will
result in being fulfilled; every man-conceived
vision will be a dead end. (Ike Reighard)*

In 2017, I published the account of our church's journey from a
monolithic congregation to a wonderful multicultural community of faith. When I moved to First Baptist Duluth in Georgia,
the church was predominantly White, nestled in the suburbs
of Atlanta. Now, it is a congregation of more than forty-five
nationalities. We titled the first book, *Technicolor*, based on an
illustration in the book's introduction related to the movie, *The
Wizard of Oz*. In the 1939 film, Dorothy, a farm girl from Kansas,
finds herself transported to the beautiful new land of Oz. I have

likened my experience of moving from the Midwestern state of Indiana to the culturally diverse area of Duluth, Georgia, in 2010 to that vibrant scene from the classic movie. The cinematic use of black-and-white film in the beginning of the story in Kansas is vividly changed when Dorothy opens the farmhouse door and sees a whole new world in Technicolor.

The Wizard of Oz was one of the earliest films to use the new cutting-edge colorization technique known as Technicolor. The movie's great success brought this pioneer process into the mainstream of film production. Movies throughout the '40s, '50s, and early '60s were now brought to the public in this new aesthetically pleasing format. This revolutionary way of creating pictures was not without its critics. As is the case in any arena of progress, change is often questioned and debated before it is eventually adopted and accepted. The producers of The Wizard of Oz may not have discovered this technology, but they were important pioneers in this new, colorful way of producing art on the screen.

In the past few years, I have become enamored with all things Technicolor. I pay close attention to any book, article, movie, documentary, or any other media source that includes the word in its title or description. Because of this newfound awareness, I discovered an intriguing TED Talk entitled "Hearing in Technicolor." My obvious curiosity was immediately piqued as I learned about a neurological condition known as synesthesia, the blending of two or more senses. With various types of synesthesia, the sound of a passing car may suddenly bring you the taste of cherry, or the touch of a cotton blanket may trigger the sound of falling rain. The word synesthesia is derived from the word synthesis. In synesthesia, senses are interconnected. I was amazed to learn that an estimated 4 percent of the population report having this remarkable condition.

One specific type of synesthesia is chromesthesia, a blending of sounds with colors or visualizations. In her TED Talk, Alexandra Hasenpflug, a millennial artist from Winnipeg, Canada, detailed her experience with chromesthesia. As she reflected on her childhood experience growing up with this "odd" ability, she revealed that she was once too embarrassed to tell anyone about it. Now, as she shares her story with the worldwide audience of the internet, the acclaimed artist claims chromesthesia as her superpower. Chromesthesia is allowing this young lady to literally *hear in technicolor*.[1]

There is some debate as to whether this condition is hereditary. Looking through her family tree, Alexandra could not find one relative known to have chromesthesia. Once, Hasenpflug's mother asked her to accompany her to the estate sale of her recently deceased Aunt Lillian. Alexandra learned that, like herself, her late aunt was also an artist. Her grieving uncle offered to show Alexandra some of her aunt's works. One particular piece spoke to Alexandra. Aunt Lillian had painted a beautiful kaleidoscope canvas that had the appearance of prisms of colors. Within the symmetric shapes she could see silhouettes of people. Alexandra showed the painting to her TED Talk audience and challenged them, "Can you see faces in the painting? Anybody?" As people examined the picture, faces appeared as if deliberately concealed by the artist in a puzzle-like fashion. Alexandra claimed that she not only could detect the faces, but she could hear them. This episode caused Alexandra to wonder at the probability that her Aunt Lillian may also have had chromesthesia.

One particular story in the New Testament mirrors this encounter. It's the story of the apostle Paul's vision to go to the Macedonians. In Acts 16:9–10, the writer says, "During the night Paul had a vision in which a Macedonian man was standing and pleading with him, 'Cross over to Macedonia and help us!' After he had seen the vision, we immediately made efforts to set out for Macedonia, concluding that God had called us to preach the gospel to them."

Paul's vision contained not just an audible reception, but also the sight of a Macedonian man, and as Paul received it, it was accompanied by a strong sense of movement in his spirit. This call captivated the apostle's heart and changed the trajectory of the early missionary movement. In a way, as God gifted the apostle with the sights and sounds and spiritual perception of this very specific invitation, Paul was *hearing in technicolor*.

Technicolor Voices Are Audible

First, Paul recognized the voice as coming from a specific individual from a specific place. The apostle's calling was not due to a demographic study or a denominational mandate. When Paul had this vision to go to Macedonia, he did not have a vision of a map of Macedonia or a mob of Macedonians crying out in mass, "Come to Macedonia!" He saw a man, an individual person from Macedonia. In my pastoral experience, I have found it's easy to say no to a map or a mob, but it's just about impossible to say no when an individual is looking you in the eye and saying, "I need help."

It's overwhelming to think that if we lined up all of the people who do not know Jesus Christ as Lord and Savior, that line would be approximately 750,000 miles long, could wrap around the earth thirty times, and is growing at a rate of 20 miles a day. Our call, however, is never about statistics, but about souls. It is always personal. There is a traditional Zulu greeting that says, "I see you." The person greeted responds: "I am here." There are people across this planet who exist in obscurity awaiting someone to say to them, "I see you."

The apostle began reasoning with the voice of the man who was standing and pleading. Do you hear the desperate cries of those who do not know Jesus as Lord today? Missionary Greg Livingston told of speaking at a large mission's conference at an American megachurch in 1979 in the midst of the Iran hostage crisis. Fifty-two Americans were being held hostage in the United States Embassy for 444 days from November 4, 1979, through January 20, 1981. Greg stood before four thousand people at the conference and asked the question: "How many of you prayed for the fifty-two Americans held hostage in Iran today?" All four thousand responded with hands up. There was total unanimity in praying for the release of the hostages in Iran. The missionary proceeded to ask a second question: "How many of you prayed for the 42 million Iranians who are under captive to their spiritual lostness and need to know Jesus Christ as Lord and Savior?" Four people were brave enough to raise their hands . . . four out of four thousand! Greg Livingstone concluded that "the American church claims to be missionary in our efforts but sometimes we close the door to those that are most needing the gospel." In the forty years since 1980, there have been more Muslims in Iran who have become believers in the Lord Jesus Christ than the previous thousand years combined. It all began when people heard the technicolor voices pleading for a people group that are without Jesus Christ.

Paul immediately responded to the voice. The Macedonian's request was "Come and help us." Americans today often suffer from what some people refer to as compassion fatigue. We have become expectant of organizations bombarding us with a litany of needs. And for the most part, these are all good things being done by good people representing good organizations: the Heart Association, the Cancer Society, and even the Girl Scouts. I know I have bought cookies that didn't fit in my diet and excused it by saying, "I am supporting a good cause!" We have heard so many people say, "Come and help us," that our hearts no longer respond to the call.

The Bible says, "If anyone has this world's goods and sees a fellow believer in need but withholds compassion from him— how does God's love reside in him?" (1 John 3:17). The phrase "withholds compassion" is translated "shutteth up his bowels of compassion" in the King James Version Bible. Some want to avoid that verse in the older English version. No one wants to talk about "bowels." However, in the first century it was commonly believed that the bowels were the place where one's emotions resided. When one felt compassion for someone, they would hurt for them, and often that hurt would be likened to an ache in the stomach, or the "bowels of compassion." Unfortunately, many today no longer feel so deeply. We see people and their needs, but we no longer empathize with them!

Technicolor Voices Are Affecting

Acts 16:10 says, "After he had seen the vision, we immediately made efforts to set out for Macedonia, concluding that God had called us to preach the gospel to them." The vision moved them to action! They immediately knew where to go and what to do! I read recently that 87 percent of Americans who own running shoes don't ever go running. Nothing is more indicting against the church than the fact that we possess the spiritual truth that all people need to hear, and yet choose not to share it. The spiritual needs of our community should move us.

These voices should not only move us but should also motivate us. Paul concluded that "God had called us to preach the gospel to them" (Acts 16:10). The Bible says in 1 Thessalonians 5:24, "He who calls you is faithful; he will do it." In 2010 at our mayor's State of the City Address, I learned that there are fifty-seven languages spoken at our local high school. Immediately, I sensed in my spirit that our church was called to take the gospel to ALL those people groups. The question is not, *if* God calls you. The question is, *when* God calls, will you do what he asks? When God called Isaiah the prophet, he recorded his response: "I heard the voice of the Lord saying, 'Whom shall I send, and who will go for Us?' Then I said: 'Here am I. Send me!'" (Isa. 6:8 NASB).

The technicolor voice of the man from Macedonia moved and motivated the apostle Paul to answer like Isaiah did. Ultimately, this voice mandated the apostle to act. Paul concluded that "God had called us to preach the gospel to them" (Acts 16:10). The reason for them to go to Macedonia was not to culturize them. The reason for them to go to Macedonia was to evangelize them. The entire intent was to take the gospel to a people who had never heard it. We must never forget that our primary task is to preach and spread the gospel.

When my first book, *Technicolor,* was published, I began receiving correspondence from across the country, primarily from church leaders desiring to learn how to effectively reach a multicultural community. One out-of-the-ordinary contact came as a Facebook message from a seventeen-year-old in Pennsylvania who was reading my book. First, I was greatly impressed that a seventeen-year-old would be reading my book. I was even more impressed that he wanted to engage me with questions about the content. I wanted to avail myself to this potential "next genera- tion" leader and offered to answer his inquiries. Obviously, this young man had a heart for evangelism and was trying to reconcile what he was reading with his current philosophy of ministry. He asked: "Shouldn't we be more concerned with evangelizing the nations rather than assimilating them into our culture?" I kindly responded: "Have you read the entire book?" The young man admitted that he had not finished the book but was very enam- ored with its premise. I encouraged him to complete the entirety of the book and offered a response to his question: "We are open to all people and all cultures not so we can brag about how many flags we have collected or how many languages are spoken in our church. On any given Sunday at First Baptist Duluth we may have people present from a Hindu, Muslim, or a Buddhist back- ground—or even from an atheistic background. These people are hearing about Jesus Christ—some for the very first time. We do what we do for one primary purpose, to tell the world about Jesus Christ. That is the mandate of the church!"

Technicolor Voices Are Altering

The encounter with the man from Macedonia altered Paul's direction in ministry. There are three clear results when one begins to hear in technicolor. First, hearing in technicolor will create unity. In Acts 16, Paul found a group of women who gathered at the river for the purpose of prayer. What is the impetus that creates the desire for people to gather at your church? I am often asked the secret of creating a church where Africans and Asians, Islanders and indigenous locals, Latinos and legacy members, and millennials and mature senior adults worship together. What creates this incredible atmosphere of unity? Every culture and every generation need the message of Jesus Christ! First Baptist Duluth honors international cultures so that we may invite people from those cultures to join us in the ultimate celebration of Christ. No matter one's cultural background, our desire is to meet at the cross and to become fellow followers of Jesus.

Hearing in technicolor will also create opportunity. The story in Acts indicates that among the ladies gathered for prayer, Lydia "opened her heart to pay attention" (Acts 16:14 ESV). Answering the technicolor call created a gospel encounter with everlasting results. The goal of the church is not to see how many worship songs we can sing in different languages. The goal for any church is for people to come to Jesus Christ. Following the direction of the technicolor voice created an open door of opportunity. Gospel conversations happen when one is attentive and responsive to the inviting voices of technicolor.

Paul's encounter with a Macedonian man teaches us that technicolor voices create multiplication in discipleship. After Lydia became a believer, she invited Paul to come to her house to visit with her friends who had never heard about Jesus Christ! Whenever someone comes to Christ, they are connected to a score of others who need to hear the gospel message. The law of multiplication is mind blowing. If one adds 2 + 2 + 2 . . . 20 times, you get a sum of 40. However, if one multiplies 2 x 2 x 2 . . . 20 times, the sum is more than 2 million. If every church member would take the attitude of Lydia to examine their circle of friends and acquaintances who need to hear about Jesus Christ and then invite them to hear the good news of Jesus, that line of people who need to know Jesus would begin to shorten, no longer stretching for hundreds of thousands of miles.

Having piqued my attention with new information about chromesthesia, I began to do additional research about the phenomenon. I found a second TED Talk by a teenager with chromesthesia named Annie Dickinson. She says everyone's voice has an accompanying color for her. As she gets to know the person better, sometimes the color associated with that person will change. A deepening of understanding about a person's likes, dislikes, and values will at times change the hue of that person's corresponding color. Annie concludes her TED Talk challenging listeners to experience diversity and perceive the colors of our society. "We must learn to listen with an open mind and hear the voices of those around us," she said.[2] It is not enough to say, "I see you." It is vital to advance to, "I hear you." The apostle Paul not only saw a man from Macedonia; he also *heard* him. He heard his heart and knew that he needed Jesus Christ. As a pastor, my desire is to lead my church not only to see the diversity of our community but to hear the heart of the people around us. And as our understanding of these new friends deepens, it will change the way we interact with them.

This book is a way to help us listen closely and learn from those technicolor voices. My wonderful collaborator, Darcy Wiley, has interviewed more than thirty church members and ministry partners, listening to their voices and deepening our understanding of the transition that has happened in their individual lives. My previous book chronicled what happened in our church during the period of transition to a multicultural community of faith. However, this second book exists to discuss the heart change, spiritual challenges, and altered mindsets from the perspective of the people who experienced them. I believe a deepened understanding of their stories will change the way we view the technicolor process.

There are three sections to the book: Legacies, Languages, and Leaders. First, we will tell you the story of our church's transformation from the perspective of our legacy members. These are the longest-tenured people at First Baptist Duluth. Often, leaders ask: "How did you get senior adults on board for a change this substantial?" Many are surprised to learn that some of our eldest members were our greatest champions for change once they understood the reason for the change and how the change would make the church more effective in reaching our community.

The second section highlights the perspective of our language members. Some of the megachurches in our area are technically "multicultural" churches. Dr. Michael O. Emerson defines a multicultural church as having 20 percent attendance from a non-majority culture group. By definition, these megachurches fit that criteria. However, for the most part, the diversity in these congregations is comprised of second- and third-generation immigrants. Many of them have little connection with their native language, and their only connection to their culture is through their parents or grandparents. At First Baptist Duluth, most of our international members are first-generation immigrants. Many of them are learning English or trying to increase their proficiency in the language. They are intimately tied to their native culture, and some profoundly miss their homeland. For many of these people, First Baptist Duluth is their first experience outside of their culture-centric or language-centric church. This section explores the factors that would motivate a first-generation immigrant to step outside of their comfort zone and become a part of a multicultural movement.

The final section of the book communicates the perspective of church leaders, community leaders, and denominational leaders. Part of the First Baptist Duluth story includes the development of a staff team that shares the heartbeat to reach our local community with the gospel and supports the changes necessary to become a multicultural congregation. The uncommon nature of our church has garnered the attention of the leaders of the community. And denominational leaders have sought information on how to replicate this type of transformational church ministry in other areas of diverse populations.

The interview process has revealed a distinctive pathway to change for each of these groups, leading them to adopt a technicolor view of ministry. There are nine steps to technicolor thinking. Every group's path is unique, yet they arrive at the same conclusion. The following pages will reveal the pattern of mindset shifts necessary to accomplish a united ministry that embraces every nation, tribe, and tongue within your community. My prayer as you read this book is that you will have your ears tuned to better hear the cry of your own "man of Macedonia" and lead others to travel this path to unity in diversity.

SECTION ONE

Legacies

Observation | Apprehension | Exhortation

Repetition | Realization | Integration

Stabilization | Appreciation | Multiplication

▼ ▼ ▼

CHAPTER ONE

A Compelling Reason

Observation | Apprehension | Exhortation

Remember the days of old; consider the years of past generations. Ask your father, and he will tell you, your elders, and they will teach you. (Deuteronomy 32:7)

When we want to know God's will, there are three things which always concur: the inward impulse, the Word of God, and the trend of circumstances. Never act until these three things agree. (F. B. Meyer)

One of the great joys of pastoring a multicultural church is learning the diverse traditions that our people adhere to from their homeland. When Pastor Abioye Tela brought his family from Nigeria to Atlanta in June of 2017 to begin his doctorate degree and ministry internship with our multicultural congregation, a contingency from our church welcomed them at the airport. We had strategically thought about what our new neighbors might like to eat for their first meal in America. Our sizable group decided to stop at Kentucky Fried Chicken for dinner before making the hour trip from the airport to Duluth. After all, chicken is the universal food! (One year, I had actually eaten Kentucky Fried Chicken in four different countries!) Abioye told our staff that the difference between Americans and Africans is that Americans eat rice with their chicken and Africans eat chicken with their rice.

The Telas would be living at our home for their first two weeks in the country. The church had secured an apartment for them, but it would not be available until the first of the month. We entered our driveway and welcomed our African friends as our houseguests. Due to the length of their travel, the entire family was off to bed rather quickly. But the next morning, as Glenda and I announced that breakfast was served and that our guests could come whenever they were ready, Pastor Abioye and his wife Joke's (pronounced Joe-Kay) young children, Aanu and Anjola, bounced down the stairs like typical five- and seven-year-olds. Immediately, Pastor Abioye appeared with Joke and instructed the children in their native Yoruba. Before I knew it, the children were lying at our feet with their faces to the ground, totally prostrate before Glenda and me. Abioye and Joke then walked toward us and each bowed down and touched our feet. Abioye explained that it is the custom in his country to honor one's elders in such a way. This display of homage is not saved for special ceremonies but is carried out daily in their home culture. Age is of such value in their background that "elder" would be defined as anyone older than yourself, even if only by one day.

As I encouraged the Telas to return to their feet, I told them that this would not be expected by elder people in their new location. However, the heart behind the gesture has formed a lasting impression on me.

I was taught by my parents the biblical principle of respect for my elders. During my nearly forty years of pastoral ministry and in every aspect of my life, I have attempted to honor this admonition. Now, I am becoming one of the "elders." At times, people overlook or dismiss the aged population in a community, but I have seen God work in a great way among my church's longest-tenured members. The first section of this book is to share the incredible story of transition among this group that I commonly refer to as our legacy members. Every person in this group has been at the church for a minimum of twenty years. These amazing people have offered wisdom, perspective, and stability in the midst of a dramatically changing environment.

When I get the opportunity to share our church's technicolor story in conferences or consultation settings, the one question that always arises is: "How did you keep your senior adults engaged during the transition?" Many are surprised to learn that this remarkable generation, rich in leadership capacity and experience, are among the captains of change in our church. However, this group has lived long enough to know that not ALL change is good. And change for the sake of change is not something you'll see them seeking out. But this generation is looking for compelling reasons that warrant change. This is their discovery of those compelling reasons.

Step One: Observation

One would have to be living in a bubble not to recognize the national change that has happened in America. We are living in an increasingly diverse society. Demographer William Frey reports that there is unprecedented ethnic and cultural change that is transforming the United States. Frey estimates that, according to current growth patterns, the United States will be "majority-minority" by the year 2050 (meaning that no one group will comprise 50 percent of the population). The fastest growth rates in minority groups are with Asians (102%), Hispanics (121%), and those that identify with two or more ethnicities (191%). Frey refers to these three groups as the "new minorities" that are reshaping the face of America.[3] In the 2010 census, Duluth had already arrived at "majority-minority" status. Duluth Mayor Nancy Harris realizes that our county is a generation ahead of the national curve. "The way Gwinnett County looks now is the way the entire United States is predicted to look by the year 2050,"[4] Harris says. When speaking to other government leaders, Harris notices an increasing interest in how our city is handling diversity, promoting unity, and creating workable solutions.

The changing demographic of America has resulted in churches that lack stability. Church growth expert Thom Rainer says, "Several thousand churches are closing each year. The pace will accelerate unless our congregations make some dramatic changes."[5] What changes need to be made to stop this statistical slide? Rainer says that one such change is for the church to adequately reflect the ethnic, racial, and socioeconomic makeup of the community. Churches where the members drive in from neighboring areas likely know little about the spiritual needs of the church's community.

Our legacy members have not only seen national change but have experienced nearby change in the city of Atlanta. In 1966, there were 166 Southern Baptist churches inside the Atlanta perimeter. Of those 166, there are only 31 churches that still exist today. In the '70s, '80s, and '90s, inner city neighborhoods changed, and many White church members moved to the suburbs in predominantly homogeneous communities. As church members moved to the outskirts, many left their inner-city church pews empty, leaving the remaining members with the responsibility of keeping up the building, programs, and local ministries with depleted tithes and offerings. Some churches kept their suburban attendees but eventually felt the pull to move to the areas that their current membership now called home. The historic First Baptist Church of Atlanta is one of those, relocating from their church facilities in the heart of the city to their current site just outside the perimeter in 1997. Bell South Corporation bought the downtown property with the thought of preserving it as a cultural center housing the city's symphony orchestra, but talks came to nothing and they ended up leveling the historic structure to put an office building in its place.

Wilbur Brooks remembers growing up as a small-town Georgia boy hungry for God's Word. Week after week he'd turn the knob on his radio ever so slightly to tune in to a favorite broadcast out of Baptist Tabernacle in downtown Atlanta. Soon, a familiar voice would come through the fabric-covered speakers, and the rich, resonant tone of Morgan Blake's voice would hit the airwaves. Morgan was a men's Bible teacher at the Baptist

Tabernacle and hosted a businessmen's Bible study in downtown Atlanta that regularly attracted more than one hundred key leaders of the city. Wilbur turned up the volume on the radio and sat down to open his Bible and be discipled through the ministry of this long-established church that burgeoned with more than three thousand members in the 1950s. Wilbur grew in his faith through the thriving outreach of that Atlanta church. But sadly, he would, one day, turn the dial to that same place on the radio and hear nothing but static.

By the 1980s, the "white flight" phenomenon had whittled the Baptist Tabernacle down to five hundred members. The changes left the church with dwindling resources that forced it to discontinue its wide-reaching programs in the congregation and the community. In 1994, the church went from decline to death when the mere one hundred remaining members voted to sell the building to House of Blues and cease to exist as a congregation. Today, the historic building is owned by another live performance and venue operating company. Wilbur is now in his nineties and is the only remaining World War II veteran at First Baptist Duluth. He is still active in our church and teaches the eldest senior adult Sunday school class. His class represents decades of wisdom from legacy members' life with Christ. "The Baptist Tabernacle is now a nightclub. That's what happens when you don't reflect the community," Wilbur laments. "I have seen things change in downtown Atlanta, and if we want to maintain our church here, we're going to have to change, and we're going to have to see our congregation reflect the same makeup as the community."

Our legacy members had not only observed national change and lived through the nearby change of the city of Atlanta, but

they were now being confronted with the personal nature of
neighborhood change. First Baptist Duluth reaped the benefit of the evacuating Baptists from downtown churches. Urban
Atlanta's pattern of church decline had brought rising attendance
to churches in many of the surrounding municipalities, including
ours. By the mid-'90s, First Baptist Duluth was being recognized
as one of the fastest-growing churches in the suburbs. One of
the church's longest-tenured staff members, Keith Murdock,
came to serve in 1997 during the zenith of growth for the fellowship. Pastor Keith was brought to Duluth to render expertise
in establishing two worship services and two Sunday schools in
order to accommodate the rapid growth. The senior pastor at the
time, Dave Parker, had come to Duluth after long-term service
as a missionary in Zambia with the International Mission Board.
Members of First Baptist Duluth easily caught his vision for international and local missions and gave more than $500,000 a year to
mission causes. The church was also engaged in funding church
planting in Atlanta and around the world with gifts of $80,000 a
year. First Baptist Duluth was a healthy, vibrant, catalytic church
in the suburbs. Growing numbers indicated a thriving church.
Yet no one realized just how delicate the statistics were under the
surface.

The population of the county continued to grow, but all of a
sudden, the church itself stalled in its numbers, dropping eighty
to ninety people a year in attendance. The church leadership
hadn't changed. The church programming that had previously
met the needs of the membership had continued. But observation of the sanctuary and classrooms left an eerie sense of loss,
as if half the people were out of town on vacation every week.

Perplexed, Senior Pastor Dave Parker asked Keith to form a task force to figure out the cause behind these unexpected changes.

No one understood it at the time, but the church's health was entirely dependent upon the migration patterns of the White middle-class majority that made up the congregation. The young families who had moved to Duluth for its attractive schools and neighborhoods were now getting eyes for towns to the north where they could get larger, newer, and nicer houses. The starter homes they left behind were beginning to be occupied by people from a variety of different ethnicities. International interest in the area had surged after Atlanta hosted the 1996 Olympics. Duluth was about to become one of the most rapidly diversifying areas of the country.

First Baptist Duluth, a missional church with a heart for ministry, was now itself losing numbers. The church sought out a consultant from the denomination to lead them in ascertaining next steps in their new normal. One day, the consultant brought in a stack of charts and graphs and a laptop with some fancy demographic software that enabled him to compare and contrast the characteristics of the people inside the church with the people living in the surrounding radius of the neighborhoods. Keith remembers the tension in the room when the demographer said, "You're in the exact wrong place to be. The people who are easy for you to reach have moved north of you. Nobody who is easy for you to reach lives around you." This conclusion was based upon the "homogeneous unit principle" that postulates that people are more likely to attend a church where they do not have to cross a racial, linguistic, or class barrier. In other words, the prospect of maintaining a ministry presence in Duluth would require the difficult task of learning how to share the gospel across these barriers. Things were changing. The trend in church decline had not stopped with urban Atlanta. Our community grew in numbers while many long-established churches declined. The consultant warned, "I know of no other church with your kind of demographics that survived. The only question that you must ask yourself is not *if* you're going to move, but *when* you are going to move. Your members are already leaving . . ."

The seismic demographic shift had reached the suburbs. Tom Jones, a retired Southern Baptist missionary to Kenya, relocated to the Duluth area. The Joneses purchased their home in 1997 while on an extended furlough. They went back to the mission field and then later returned to their chosen retirement spot in 2006. Upon his return, he observed the incredible change that had taken place in less than a decade. "Our house was located in a cul-de-sac with a total of fifteen homes. When we bought the house in 1997, the entire neighborhood was Anglo. When we returned in 2006, only five of the fifteen homes were occupied by Anglo families. The houses on both sides of ours were occupied by families from India. (Interestingly, our daughter and son-in-law were serving as missionaries in India at the time.) Across the street was an African American family. There were also several Korean families among us. I asked myself the question: 'What is the local church going to do to reach this community?'"

Not only had the demographic shift reached our suburban neighborhoods, but so had the trend of church closings. Each year, additional fellowships would close their doors or sell their facilities to another congregation. Some relocated, others merely ceased to exist. First Baptist Duluth leaders observed this trend move up the Interstate 85 corridor into the northern suburbs like a plague. Life-and-death choices were now affecting our nearest neighboring churches. One of First Baptist Duluth's longest-tenured members is Charles Summerour, who has been affiliated with the church the entirety of his seventy years of life. Charles is a local historian who has observed, firsthand, the changes in the community and in the church. Charles said, "Look at the history of this area. You start south of us and there is church closing after church closing. And I'm not talking about just any churches, but 'First' Baptist Churches! Until the church just six miles from our church closed . . ." This trend of church closure seemed to be headed directly toward us.

Founded in 1886, our church was well over a hundred years old at the time these community changes began taking place. We had a lot to lose. Many of our members had been born in the community, raised in the church, and had married and raised their own families here. When the congregation had outgrown its small stone sanctuary in the center of town in the late '70s, Charles Summerour's grandfather-in-law sold the church a large piece of property to begin construction on our current church building. This was a tight-knit community. Generations of families have invested their lives in the discipleship and ministry of First Baptist Duluth. Now the supposed experts were telling the congregation they had to move the church out of Duluth in order to survive. What would First Baptist Duluth be without Duluth? And, what would Duluth be without First Baptist Duluth?

In the midst of the pressure to move and forfeit ministry in the community that had been the church's home since its inception, Pastor Dave Parker publicly stated, "We're staying. We're not moving. We're not running." Be that as it may, Parker was getting ready to retire from pastoring and return to the mission field. While he vocalized the decision to stay in the midst of an ever-changing Duluth, it would be up to the people left behind to determine next steps. First Chronicles 12:32 (NIV) sheds light on a group of King David's supporters in a time of uncertainty, "from Issachar, men who understood the times and knew what Israel should do—200 chiefs, with all their relatives under their command." Staff member Keith says that in one way, the church leaders and members felt like the sons of Issachar—they understood the times. But they were missing the last half of the equation. They didn't know what to do. For churches living through demographic changes like the one in Duluth, the only model up to that point was "stay and die out." Now that the decision had been made to stay in place, First Baptist Duluth had to decide if they were going to accept the typical fate of dying or step up and do something different. They didn't know what to do, but doing nothing was not an option.

When I arrived as pastor of First Baptist Duluth in 2010, I admit I did not know exactly what to do. In my previous book, *Technicolor*, I share my experience of moving to Duluth from a homogeneous Midwestern community. When we unloaded our belongings into our new home, my wife, Glenda, and I set out to meet our neighbors. Next door was a delightful cross-cultural couple, a Malaysian husband and a Vietnamese wife. On the other side of our house was a family from India. Our neighbors behind us were from Korea. Across the street from us was a young family from Zimbabwe. At the end of our street was an oral surgeon from Puerto Rico, and across the street from them was a multigenerational family from Nigeria. In short, the predominantly White congregation that I now served looked nothing like the neighborhood where I now lived!

One of the Sunday school classes had a dinner to welcome me as the newly arriving pastor. The class teacher hosted the gathering in his home. He quieted the crowd to say the blessing and offer a word of welcome to my wife and me. The most memorable part of this evening was him asking me before we prayed, "What can we do for you to make your ministry here successful?" I replied, "Allow me the opportunity to fail." There were no models or step-by-step task lists for a transition like this. We began trying things, building on what we already had. In our "on-the-job training," we've made our share of discoveries of what works well and what doesn't work well in our situation. I hope these lessons and insights can be a gift to churches across the nation to fill in the second half of the sons-of-Issachar equation. You understand the times; now here's a way to do something with that knowledge.

Step Two: Apprehension

It's not a surprise that the situation we found ourselves in brought a great deal of uncertainty. As members observed the reality of what had happened to many churches like ours, they were faced with the fear of death. One of our legacy members, Leland Strange, a pragmatic businessman, studied the decline of the Atlanta churches and said, "Based upon the previous trajectory of First Baptist Duluth, given the size of the building, the fixed expenses, and the dwindling congregation, I estimated that we would not survive more than ten to fifteen years doing what we were doing before." Many of our long-tenured members were extremely concerned about the viability of their church. Was First Baptist Duluth headed toward the same fate as neighboring congregations? Were the health issues of the church a reversible trend? Or was the demise of the church a forgone conclusion?

It may surprise you that fear of death is a lousy motivational tool. Writer Alan Deutschman has an enlightening article titled "Change or Die" (later expanded and published into a book by the same title). Deutschman reports that when ten people are confronted with the prospects that they must change their behavior in order to survive (e.g., stop smoking, eat less salt, exercise daily), nine of them will choose NOT to change. They value their current preferences in life over cultivating a long, healthy life.[6] Just as people refuse to change to avoid physical death, I have observed some churches that are unwilling to change in order to avoid the church's death. As strange as it seems, the fear of death alone will seldom change the direction of a congregation headed toward demise.

It seems that, for some, even more powerful than the fear of death is the fear of something different. College professor and motivational speaker Scott Mautz points out that "change" elicits a natural discomfort in our lives. We fear things that are different because of the uncertainty that they bring. Podcaster Tim Ferris claims, "People would rather be unhappy than uncertain." Neuroscience research has indicated that "uncertainty" registers in the brain in the same manner as "error" does. Therefore, things that are different are physiologically perceived as wrong.[7]

Senior adults knew about the demographic changes in the community. They could hear other languages spoken in the grocery aisles and see unfamiliar lettering on signs for local businesses or for language-centric churches. But since Duluth is dotted with a plethora of churches specifically started by and for a particular culture or language group, many legacy members questioned why we would need to reach out to our international neighbors. In the nicest voice possible with sincere curiosity, those senior adults would ask: "Why don't those people go to their *own* church?" If there was a church specifically designed to meet their needs located down the street, why did we need to get involved? It may be hard for some who are naturally less resistant to imagine that these legacy members cared about the souls and lives of all people, but it is true. Though they had a heart for seeing all nations know the love of Christ, they had never considered that *they* might actually be the ones to share the gospel or disciple others who didn't look like them. In their eyes, only a missionary specially trained for cross-cultural ministry or a person native to one of those other cultures could be equipped for walking alongside these new international neighbors.

Retired missionary Tom Jones summarized it this way: "Old folks, like I am now, often resist change. They just want stability. Anything that disrupts their lives is a problem for them." If we were to interview the senior adults and ask if they agree with the way our church is reaching our community, they would know the politically correct response is "yes." That is in keeping with the things they've been taught from Scripture and even their own sense of hospitality and etiquette. But then there's the heart response that comes through in the facial expression, mannerisms, or interactions. There is discomfort there, and discomfort often acts out as rigidity. So, how do you get a group of people who are innately resistant to change to try something different?

There are many layers to the apprehension that our legacy members felt toward the changes around us, but we weren't going to get anywhere by telling them what to think. We had to help them discover and navigate the issues themselves and arrive at their own God-inspired conclusion. Hypothetically, if one of our members were to garner the courage to share Christ with an immigrant in the community and see that person become a new believer, it's hard to picture those legacy members maintaining their segregated tone and proclaiming, "You can't come to my church. You've got to go to worship with your kind of people." None of our people would openly propagate such an idea. As people began to ask their questions aloud and hear their own thoughts in contrast to the mission of the church, the options became clear. Did we really want to reach our community, or in our desire for familiarity and comfort did we want to die out, leaving ministry undone in Duluth?

The fear of the church's death and the fear of something different were joined by the final piece of the fear triangle. For our legacy members, there was a fear of dissipation. As the tight-knit community of Duluth was now becoming home to a new wave of immigrants who had not grown up in the culture, long-tenured residents were feeling as if they were "losing control" of their community and their church. Virginia Jones, who has lived in Duluth since 1976, says, "I loved the way it was in the '60s and '70s and '80s. Not that I was against the new people, because I really love all people, but it broke my heart to see some of the changes."

One of the most difficult transitions within our congregation had to do with the changes in our worship music. This is as much a generational issue as it is a cultural issue, and many churches across the United States struggle to find a way to connect both the young and the old through the musical styles used in the worship service. Many of our senior adults feared that we'd lose the formal beauty of our choir and orchestra. Contemporary music style was enough of a stretch for them, so when we began to incorporate music with other languages, many of our senior adults didn't feel at home anymore.

Virginia recalls how we began to incorporate elements from other cultures into our church services and activities, like a traditional fan dance from South Korea. She and some of her friends feared that the traditions they once held dear from the church's past were now being forgotten and replaced by these unfamiliar traditions. They felt that deference always seemed to be in favor of the newcomers. In essence, they feared that they were being overlooked. Virginia said, "In the beginning, I was very against it because it seemed like we were changing over and giving in to them. My main objection was that I thought we were changing our church more to their culture and thus losing some of our American culture."

While these legacy members would stand against obvious instances of racism and injustice, and they considered themselves to be caring and compassionate people, they were still uncomfortable with the changing atmosphere around them. They were largely unfamiliar with other cultures, and a lack of familiarity can often feel like fear. Lindsay Lapole, a retired executive of the Salvation Army who served us as a deacon, Sunday school teacher, and longtime chairman of the stewardship committee, says, "We have to come nose to nose with how prejudiced we are. It's not prejudice in the traditional sense. It looks more like being set in our ways." Lindsay says this shows up in the seemingly harmless form of personal preference. We may be uncomfortable with different ways of greeting each other and may not know how to conduct ourselves in the awkward silences or misspeaks between languages. We may not appreciate the aromas that come from another culture's home cooking, or we may not be familiar with the smell of certain health and beauty products as we hug or shake a hand. Suddenly, all the things that our members could once do without thinking now came with uncertainty, second-guesses, and self-consciousness.

As our legacy members stepped into this feeling of unfamiliarity, one of the things that helped most was to bring their attention back to familiar things that unite us. It was vital that we focused together on the things we will never leave behind that, in turn, give us a reason to step forward. The key component that has galvanized our legacy members in overcoming these fears is the always familiar Great Commission: "Go, therefore, and make disciples of all nations, baptizing them in the name of the Father and of the Son and of the Holy Spirit" (Matt. 28:19). There are no Great Commission exemptions. We know God has strategically placed us in this community. The community has rapidly diversified and changed. Therefore, God in His abundant wisdom must want us to reach a diverse community.

Virginia Jones shares how she overcame her own apprehensions: "I would now say that as our neighbors are changing, we want them to come to our church. We need to accept them. We need to welcome them. We need to be able to witness to them. Our witness is what is most important. We do not ever want to turn people away." The familiar thing that guided our legacy members through uncertainty and apprehension was simply and consistently bringing their attention back to the things they already knew to be true.

Step Three: Exhortation

Good theology creates unity. I regularly preach on the theme of Christ's call to minister to the nations. However, with the legacy members, it was less about *teaching* them these biblical admonitions and more about *reminding* them. Legacy members have a wealth of biblical knowledge and spiritual insight to offer in this discussion. Paying closer attention to God's Word, our existing members began to see that our church in these times was in a unique position to demonstrate the love and power of God in a spectacular way. Why are we here, if not to reach the people within our local community? Lindsay Lapole explains: "You have to have a biblical perspective of what church is about. It is broader than just 'Jesus loves me, this I know, for the Bible tells me so.' You must at some point dig into the scriptural understanding personally. At some point, one must separate cultural preferences from biblical truth."

With the Great Commission as our driving force, we began to ask: "What would Christ have us do?" As we consciously established Scripture as our instruction for how to move forward, our members began to make connections between what we were seeing in our everyday ministry and the wisdom God had already equipped us with in His Word. As particular situations would arise, whether with the changes around us or the conflict in our hearts and between the different ways of thinking among us, our senior adults would recall a biblical teaching that addressed the need. The prayer of Jesus in John 17 explains that our unity in the midst of diversity is a testimony of God's power to the world. As we studied this passage together, one legacy member said succinctly, "Good theology creates unity." God's Word was giving us anthems to guide us through the work set before us.

It was rewarding to watch people, after personal introspection, embrace ministries that promoted multicultural interaction. Wilbur Brooks, who teaches Sunday school to the eldest group of senior adults, described the transformation among his peers: "I have seen some who resisted the change at first. Now, they are sold on the program. I think the shift came when they read their Bible and they could see this is what God is wanting us to do." Wilbur alluded to the calling in Acts 1:8 that we should be witnesses "to the ends of the earth." This incredible leader among the legacy members is constantly reminding people that this path to becoming a church that reflects and includes our international community is actually just a group of God's people being obedient to the calling to be a New Testament church.

But this model of the New Testament church has for too many years been overshadowed by faulty ways of thinking in the Baptist denomination. For decades, church strategists were locked in on the concept of the homogeneous church: Anglos with Anglos, Hispanics with Hispanics, Koreans with Koreans, and so on and so forth. Retired missionary Tom Jones observed that this methodology is not at all in line with the model of the

New Testament church. He points out that the first indication of a cross-cultural church is the church of Jerusalem in Acts 6. The reason for the selection of the first deacons was to heal a rift in this multicultural fellowship. Turn the pages to go a few chapters forward in Acts and you'll read the names of Antioch church leaders from five different nationalities who sent Paul out on his first missionary journey. The early church described in the Bible was clearly founded as a multicultural fellowship.

Knowing that the Scriptures clearly teach a calling to multicultural work, some legacy members were also asking: "What does my conscience say?" Not all of our members were as apprehensive about the cultural changes around us that would soon be seen in our church. Some of them have had extensive exposure to people from different cultural backgrounds. Some have been involved in advocating for even more daunting changes in their past.

As a college student in the 1960s, Leland Strange was a member of a downtown Atlanta church. Desiring to make change from within, Leland showed up with a group from Georgia Tech to help his Black peers find a way inside the building to worship in the Whites-only sanctuary. As he remembers the passion he and his friends had for Atlanta-area integration efforts, he smiles and calls his younger self a rabble-rouser. Whatever the time or place, Leland says, "Every day you just get up and do what you ought to do. We took it upon ourselves to try to find a way to get them into the church, some kind of door where they could get in." But church leaders barred the doors that friends like Leland had hoped to open. Onlookers shouted as leaders escorted the young Black men down the steps and ushered them off the property.

The message was clear to the young Black men and their friends who stood for their biblical and civil right to worship in the same places as the majority population: *you're not welcome*. In solidarity with his peers of another color, Leland reached through the linked arms of the white deacons, cheerfully shook the hand of a Black student, and said, "I'm glad you're here." Leland felt the pushback immediately as the white men blocked Leland and began to pummel him with their fists. Later, he and half a dozen friends sat down to chat with the pastor of the church, a man who had also held the highest office in the convention. While the pastor's heart seemed soft to the integration efforts of the day, his issue was his deacons, old Southern folks who wouldn't budge on their prejudices. Leland believes if it hadn't been for that peer pressure, the pastor would have opened the doors once and for all. I guess compared to the hardened hearts and fists of those deacons in the 1960s, facing the fears and frustrations of church members during our community transition hasn't felt so difficult for Leland! At various times in his life, Leland has found himself as a go-between, bridging two ways of thinking.

It's important to have people like Leland in a congregation that is dealing with change. For him, this bridging involved a lot of what he calls "Waffle House meetings." In these meetings, Leland would spend time sitting with friends who were trying to make sense of the changes in the community and the future of their church. Both in his younger years and in recent times, Leland has used his voice to help others see the biblical and civil importance of being a good neighbor. "You need some mediation. You need some folks who will understand both sides." Like Leland, several of our senior adults with more exposure and experience with other cultures have stepped in to be a bridge between their hesitant peers and the way God has opened for us to move forward.

The legacy members rediscovered the biblical principles of ministering to "all people." Many of them consulted their conscience and found a compelling voice reiterating the "right thing to do." After asking, "What does Christ say?" and "What does my conscience say?" Now, they were beginning to ask: "What does common sense say to do?" First Baptist Duluth is a historically mission-minded church that now finds itself in the midst of one of the most diverse communities in America. We believe with all our heart the calling of the Great Commission to take the gospel to "all nations" (Matt. 28:19). And here the nations have become our very own neighbors. Common sense says we need to keep our legacy of ministry alive in this very spot on the map and we do so by including our neighbors.

At those Waffle House meetings, Leland would empathize with his friends' apprehensions, saying that he missed the old style of music, too. But then, he would bring the conversation around to the higher purpose: "But it's not about me. It's not about you. It's about God. Now what can we do to keep this church in place fifty years from now? It's not just about the people who were here before or are here right now. It's about what's going to serve God over the long haul. We want to see the church survive and meet the needs of our local community."

Many of those friends accepted that call to a new way of being the church and are watching as God, even in their twilight years, works in them in a whole new way. Together, we have observed the changing dynamics in the community around our church, we have begun to work through apprehensions within our church, and we have committed ourselves once again to depending on Scripture as a filter for everything we face. Together, we are coming to see that these challenges before us are actually an opportunity to perform in our own community the ministry we have always prioritized in the world.

CHAPTER TWO

▼ ▼ ▼

Time to Reset

Repetition | Realization | Integration

Make your ways known to me, LORD; teach me your paths.
Guide me in your truth and teach me.
(Psalm 25:4–5)

Attempt great things for God and expect great things from God.
(William Carey)

When I went to the hospital to pray with Cecil Nash before his heart surgery, I had no idea of the events that were getting ready to unfold. Cecil was one of our more vocal legacy members, resistant to the changes taking place. I knew of Cecil's hesitance about our church's vision for inviting the international community around us into our congregation, but I felt no tension toward him. Though he didn't understand or embrace the new calling of our church, I loved him as my brother in Christ and a treasured member of my church community. I trusted that just as I, myself, and we at First Baptist Duluth are a work in progress as a congregation, Cecil and his friends with all their concerns and fears are a work in progress, as well. As Cecil and I lifted our heads from prayer and I watched the doctors wheel him behind the doors to begin the surgery, I said, "You're going to come through just fine. I know God has more work for us to do together."

I don't know all of the ins and outs of what went wrong, but somewhere in the middle of Cecil's heart procedure, they lost him. The beeps on the monitor slid into a sustained alarm sound and the nurses scattered to grab the defibrillator. For minutes on end, which can seem like days in an emergency situation like that, the doctors and nurses worked on his heart but saw no fruit from their labor. Cecil was dead. Still, the medical personnel continued squeezing the heart and shocking it, using every resource they had to try to get it pumping again. Another jolt of electricity and then, after five whole minutes of uncertainty, the monitor began to beep in a steady rhythm. The whole room full of hospital staff breathed a sigh of relief as, on that operating table, Cecil began to breathe again.

What happened that day was a reset for Cecil, both physically and spiritually. Cecil had always prided himself in having a memory like a steel trap. If you'd rattle off a phone number, he'd never need a pen and paper or need to type the contact information into his phone. He would simply store the numbers in his own memory bank for the next time he needed to call. He remembered family birth dates and anniversaries by heart and never forgot a name. Our church members and returning visitors can attest to this. But when the brain is without oxygen for a few minutes, a person is likely to experience some changes. After a cardiac arrest incident, the patient may have trouble with anything ranging from muscle control to memory recall. When Cecil showed signs of some mild memory loss, his doctor prescribed memory therapy to reprogram his brain.

For many months following the surgery, Cecil worked through a long series of modules in a special computerized program to help him regain his capacity to embrace new information. This memory therapy involves much repetition, interacting with the same example from a variety of different angles until the brain can adequately absorb the content and create a better foundation for future memory retention. Like using weights to tone or strengthen a certain set of muscles through repeated movements, this program is a workout for the brain. As Cecil participated in these exercises and walked the long road to recovery, he came to view his experience as a metaphor for the larger work God is doing in him individually as well as in our church body as a whole.

Step Four: Repetition

When changes come in a life or in a community, it is natural for those involved to feel disoriented for some time. Just as Cecil had to become acclimated to a new way of learning and interacting after his medical procedure, the legacy members of our church were faced with many unknowns that made them feel out of their element. As we walked forward in the call to becoming a multicultural church, some were upset and even questioned the motives of the leadership, but we knew our legacy members

already had the capacity to love those from very different backgrounds than their own.

For some legacy members, their first exposure was a positive relationship with a fellow church member from a different
background, a relationship that set the groundwork for a new
way of thinking. One senior adult ladies' class had the privilege
of doing life and ministry alongside an African American member
who had grown up in Birmingham when Bull Connor was police
chief. She graduated from a historically black college in the early
'60s, an era infamous for violent racism. White people sprayed
her people with fire hoses. White people let German shepherds
loose on her and her friends. White people wouldn't give her a
job. Yet years later, she chose to come and make herself at home
at this predominantly White church. In recent years, a study at
University of Zurich found that "being the recipient of just a few
small acts of generosity by a stranger from an outside group created neurobiological changes in the brain that made individuals
more empathetic to all members of that outside group."[8] Repeated
positive encounters overcame the gap between two very different backgrounds among our senior adult ladies. The tension that
could have existed between these women because of larger soci-
etal dysfunctions was absent. This woman and the other ladies
in her class counted each other as dear friends. Legacy members
from White backgrounds listened intently to her stories, learned
from her, and loved her deeply. They became so comfortable in
her presence that there was virtually no sense of otherness.

Similar connections were long-established throughout our
congregation. In a relaxed environment within their comfort zone
and with a common connection in Christ, church members were

glad to join with diverse friends in prayer, study, worship, and everyday conversation. Our legacy members felt at home in these intercultural friendships, but they had yet to translate them to the larger picture of community change. We could not be satisfied with these few examples of good intercultural friendships inside our walls when there were so many people from a wide variety of backgrounds not being engaged outside them.

This initial exposure was a great starting point. It was a calling to a wider, more intentional approach to connect with and meet the needs of all people within our community. Those who understood and embraced the call as early adopters had to be persistent in reminding other members of the call to reach all people while providing repeated opportunities for existing members to simply spend time with newcomers from various backgrounds and develop intercultural friendships that stretched beyond those they'd already established.

Most of us have, at one time or another, heard a song, a nursery rhyme, or catchy phrase that suddenly triggered a flood of memories, sometimes linking to scenes from as far back as our childhood. Words or melodies repeated over the course of months or years weave themselves in our memories, becoming deeply familiar to us and a part of who we are. Research has confirmed that the more a person hears something repeated, the truer it seems. And when one interacts with the new truth or reality, one begins to feel a familiarity with it. Social psychologist Robert Zajonc studied a phenomenon that he called the "mere-exposure effect." His experiments demonstrated that when a new idea is introduced, it produces an initial response of uncertainty. However, "repeated exposure can reduce such uncertainty, and thus engender more positive feelings."[9] We observed this element of human nature at work in our legacy members.

Cecil says, "Repetition is the way we as humans learn. We've had to do a lot of repetition in our church to help us old-timers understand. Through repetition, we subconsciously absorb things even when we don't want to hear it." Many legacy members expressed that repeated exposure over a long period of time softened them to the idea of a multicultural church.

Our senior adult social ministry leader, Virginia Jones, thought for a while that we acted too quickly and went overboard in the way we welcomed newcomers from various cultures. But now she sees things differently. She says, "As things went along, it seemed like there were so many changes all at once, but then we kind of got used to that. And then I could see where things were going, and the changes didn't feel as drastic. When things leveled off and the newcomers became part of us, our original group didn't feel quite as left out. Eventually, we just accepted it because we knew that was the way it was in our community and now in our church. I saw that things were working and determined that this must be what God wants. At this point, we have a lot of activities here for other cultures and I think that's great. I like to learn about other cultures." After repeated interactions with people they were once unsure of, our legacy members are becoming comfortable with our new visitors and seeing them as friends. They find joy in learning and doing ministry within a more diverse congregation.

The difficult part about repetition is that it requires patience. When a visionary discovers a new calling, self-restraint is hard, but wise leaders who have lived and served for several decades know how important it is to leave the bulldozer behind and take a more slow and steady approach. Legacy member Charles Summerour recalls that when other leaders and I realized what God was telling us, we chose to be slow and methodical, rolling out plans without going head over heels. Our businessman friend Leland Strange says, "I'm a really impatient person, but I also know that there are times when you're not going to get where you want to be if you go too fast. We had to take it slow so our legacy members wouldn't feel too much pressure." His view is that if a church has 50 percent minority population and 50 percent long-time members, the church should do ministry with 60 percent of the activities and programming meant to meet the needs and preferences of the newcomers and 40 percent meant to meet the needs and preferences of the preexisting members. If a church goes 80 percent in the direction of the newcomers and 20 percent to the longtime members, it can make it much more disorienting and difficult for the longtime members to feel connected in the changing congregation. Leland says, "You're going to defer to your future vision for the church, not the old, but you don't want to get so far ahead that things feel overboard."

As our church began to shift and address the needs of our surrounding community, we knew it would be important to craft a new mission statement. This would be the sentence repeated by the congregation again and again for years to come, reminding us to stay the course in our calling. But with tensions surrounding the changes and many senior adults feeling left out as we tended to our newcomers, it was vital that we gave ownership and voice to our legacy members, showing respect for their wisdom and perspective, so that they wouldn't be repeating this mission statement through gritted teeth.

The team tasked with crafting a new mission statement for our changing church was comprised of seven church leaders, four of whom represented our legacy members. The most debated aspect of the task came down to terminology. Because our community had become majority-minority, we needed to become a multicultural church that followed the call to reflect and reach our community. However, we also had to be careful in how we phrased this. Our ultimate goal was not to create a multicultural gathering for its own sake, but rather to effectively reach *whatever* people God had placed in the radius around us now and in the years to come, whether that meant lifelong Duluth residents or newcomers.

It may come as a surprise, but after much deliberation over the mission statement, we chose not to use the word *multicultural*. We did this to focus our hearts and minds on Jesus Himself rather than risk focusing too heavily on having a multicultural image. We emerged from our meetings with a mission statement that makes no distinction between the longtime residents of Duluth and the diverse newcomers. Our mission statement reminds all members of our highest calling, exhorting us to wholeheartedly live out the Great Commission in our city: "We are a united community of faith that loves, reaches, and disciples ALL PEOPLE for the Lord Jesus Christ." The direction is clear. The goal is biblical. This statement, crafted by a team with a majority of legacy members, was joyfully adopted by the congregation with no opposition. We continue to use this mission statement as part of our weekly services on Sundays to remind people of who we are and where we are headed.

But we went beyond words to help our long-time members get accustomed to the idea of having our diverse neighbors near. Repetition does not need to be mundane. We have found that repetition is most effective when a value or idea is presented in creative ways that engage many different senses. In this transition, existing members have tasted new flavors and heard new songs being sung and languages being spoken. They have watched cultural dances, appreciated new kinds of arts and crafts, and experienced new ways of worship.

Among our legacy members, probably the most popular of all our approaches has been the collection of flags that encircles the auditorium. The forty-seven flags represent the birth nations of every First Baptist Duluth member. In decades past, the congregation had periodically displayed the flags of the countries where missionaries had been sent out by the church. Therefore, this was something familiar to our legacy members, a tradition they were able to repurpose for a new calling. Virginia Jones represents what we've heard from many of our senior adults when she says, "I love seeing all the flags around our congregation that represent all the nations that are here." This display brings color to our auditorium and serves as a visual symbol of who we are—a united body of believers from all parts of the globe.

As new members from various backgrounds join us, we check to make sure the flag of their country of origin is represented in the lineup. And, of course, the legacy members appreciate that our own nation's flag stands alongside all the others. The permanent installation of flags that we have today represents the international work that God is doing right in our very own pews! And when visitors from represented countries join us for a worship service, our existing members have an automatic way to connect with them and let them know that they are seen, known, and appreciated.

Lasting change for people is seldom achieved by force; it comes through patient demonstration of God's Word in action. The best way to create an atmosphere of change is to provide clear examples that model the desired outcome. Legacy members sought people and processes that they could follow with confidence on this new path into the technicolor vision.

Mayor Nancy Harris, a long-time member of our congregation, says, "I know that the resistance of people in my generation and those older than me came from a lack of understanding and exposure, not out of a hardness of heart. But you must keep walking the talk. That's how you see change, I think. On Sunday mornings, I move around and sit with different people. I know that's what I'm supposed to be doing, not being cliquish. You end up hugging the same people every Sunday if you're always sitting in the same place. If you move around, you're meeting different people and shaking different hands." Something as simple as where we sit in the church service can represent our heart's posture, and that can have a profound impact on people. Am I willing to move around and see things from a different perspective or am I staking my ground in my part of the sanctuary?

When we become aware of things like this and make changes in our own everyday actions, we help model the beliefs and values we want to see take root in the broader congregation. Cecil says that by repeatedly watching leaders like Mayor Nancy and myself, he learned by example what our new calling looks like in real life. He says, "I always see Brother Mark go out and move around and talk with the new people. He's a loving person, a wonderful example. Now, I try to do what he does, too, to show through my actions that I treat everyone the same. In recent times, I've made it a point to go up to people from different backgrounds and let them know I'm thankful that they're there. You'd be surprised how many of these people open their arms and give me a hug. Maybe that's because I'm an old man, but I'll take it. That's the kind of relationship I want to have with people. And maybe seeing me do this has helped change some other people in the church, too."

As we set out to follow our new calling, many of our legacy members had only been thinking about what they were losing and what they didn't like about the changes. But as they were repeatedly presented with new people, new cultural elements, and new ways of living out the gospel, they began to see through the fog of their preferences and find a clear path forward.

In the process, they began to have confidence that those of us who had already embraced the new plan were simultaneously embracing them, our legacy members, in the family of faith. The fear of being left out and left behind began to dissipate. Leland Strange says, "You don't have to destroy the old to create the new. The new will look different from the old, but the old will show through."

The process of becoming a multicultural church has resembled on-the-job training. Even with all of our intentional planning, this has been a learning process. If I had it to do over again, knowing how difficult this was for many of our legacy members,

I would have been even more intentional from the very start to vocalize how much each existing member and their shared legacy matter to the future of our church. We wouldn't be who we are without them.

This transition was not about ignoring our history but about inviting people into our history as a family of faith, while being open to incorporating new elements too. Over time, with repeated efforts to communicate the heart and purpose of the changes, our holdouts began to sense their own worth and value to us as well as sensing the worth and value of our new calling. They began to see that these changes are not about us versus them, but about what's going to serve God best in this very spot on the map for years and decades to come.

It took many months of following an intentional plan to help acclimate our legacy members to the new life of our church, but with consistent repetition of our shared purpose, providing opportunities for interaction with real people from diverse backgrounds, and surrounding members with the beautiful symbols of our growing ministry, we saw a change in mind, heart, and behavior. Legacy members came to the realization that not only was this plan scriptural and necessary for our church's future, it was also something that they *wanted* to participate in.

Step Five: Realization

Our existing members found that after repeated experience of our new way of ministry, they now had an open mind. Cecil Nash recently told me that when we began talking about the changes we needed to make, a group of disgruntled friends had

seen him as a natural leader and tried to convince him to serve
as their spokesperson at the church's business meetings. Cecil,
however, determined he would speak only for himself. There was
always tension in the room whenever the business meeting subject
turned to discussions of new ministries aimed at reaching our
diverse community. Cecil spoke up at one such business meeting,
asking how leadership had settled on this course and why the
church hadn't been asked to vote on the initiative. I wondered
why anyone would feel the need to vote on actively pursuing and
evangelizing our community. I never had to wonder what Cecil
was thinking, though. I could count on him to tell me! Still, he
worked on striking a balance between expressing his thoughts
and concerns in a straightforward way while trying his best to be
respectful to those of us shepherding the church. He says, "Even
though I wasn't sure of the plan, what God had in store with all
this, I still could not do anything that would go against my pastor.
I knew God didn't want me to do that. I purposely went up and
talked to him and hugged him in front of those who were seeking to make me a spokesperson against the new plan. I wanted
to show them that I wasn't going to dishonor our pastor." Cecil's
relationship with me and others in leadership, his commitment to
being respectful, and his honest communication all helped him to
become more open-minded and trusting.

Part of having an open mind is letting go of the idea that
we must agree on everything in order to work together or step
forward in a new plan or purpose. Cecil says, "I don't really want
to be a leader. I want to show people how to follow. I want other
people to see that if I can do this, they can do it. I can't agree
with everything Pastor Mark does, but that's normal. If I agreed

with everything he said, I wouldn't be a person myself." Over the course of many meetings, we went through the data about the changing demographics in our neighborhoods. People could tell these details were true just by saying hi to their neighbors or pushing a cart down the aisles at the local grocery store. We examined the trajectory of dying churches versus thriving churches in similar contexts. This was also something our members were familiar with as they drove by many long-established churches that now had for-sale signs in their front yards. We shared God's heart for all people as expressed in Scripture, and this part of our discussion was always the most unifying.

Cecil and the many other existing members who endured this initial process found that the input eventually began to shift their thinking. Like so many of our treasured senior adults, this man who had once been so resistant stayed around long enough to let the changes change him. A long way from the conflicted business meetings of old, Cecil now says, "Some of these people who were so negative, the old-timers like me, are sitting back and saying, 'We're going to stay here.' There's so many—including myself—who were shocked at first, but now we understand. I have learned so much from this experience. I've become a better Christian from following this journey."

Legacy member and former missionary Tom Jones underscores how closely an open mind is linked with open ears to hear from God. Tom says that church members should, "Ask God, 'What are you trying to teach me by bringing these people into my community?' We can then realize that we won't be able to draw them to faith in Jesus Christ if we don't understand them, if we don't talk to them. Our command as Christians is to reach everybody. It didn't say just for the preachers and missionaries to go do that. Every person in the pew is supposed to. I think the key to it is having an open mind. Let God speak to you, then do what He says." This new direction in ministry has challenged us and enlivened our long-time members in the areas of personal growth and discipleship.

With new information, we have the chance not only to think differently, but to feel differently about the changing world around us. As we become more aware of our responses, we can do a spiritual heart-check and take notice of the difference between the way we see a situation and the way God sees it. Legacy member Lindsay Lapole says, "God sends us things that give us the choice to grow or retreat. You're finally going to have to decide. You have to come to grips with who He is and who you are in relationship to Him and discern if that is expressed biblically in how you relate to others. The fact is when you've got fifty-seven different languages spoken in the schools in your area, you've got to do something. We're thrust into a situation where God forces us to make a decision. Are we for Him and with Him or are we not?"

God was obviously working in the hearts of our leaders, and some of the outliers among our legacy members. Eventually, we began to see the fruit of a soft, approachable heart. Most of our legacy members who had stayed with us and weathered the transition were beginning to transition to a technicolor worldview. Charles Summerour says, "These people had every reason to rebel against the process and go and do whatever they wanted to do at another church, but it says a lot about who they are that they stayed. That doesn't mean we didn't lose a lot of friends who did decide to leave. But we've got some really good people here who have the right heart. That's what it takes. I don't think everybody likes everything, don't get me wrong. But they didn't like every-thing before, either! I enjoy seeing the senior adults who've grown to accept these changes. It's just a blessing to me to watch the pro-cess for these people who I didn't expect to become receptive."

Along with being reminded about God's purposes for the church, many of our legacy members were growing through the Holy Spirit's nudges in their personal walk with God. Senior adult ministry leader Virginia Jones recalls a devotional about the "grouchy mouth" that affected her: "We gripe, and we grumble and complain, and then with that same tongue we praise God. Griping and praise should not come from the same mouth." She came to accept that God was involved in this change and began to trust Him in it. "This must be what God wants. Who am I to object? And since I know that God is in control, I decided to accept it and stop griping. I did a lot of griping in the beginning."

There have been several phases in the transformation of our legacy members, and in Cecil's personal transformation. At first Cecil went from being resistant to not caring whether this new plan worked for our church—he felt he could always leave the church and attend somewhere else. But now, Cecil says that see-ing God's work among the nations here has made him more aware and interested in the overseas work of our church and in the lives of people in faraway lands. Recently, when we handed out a pamphlet about an upcoming ministry trip to India, Cecil noticed his change of heart: "In the past, I wouldn't pay any attention to something like that because I didn't really care that much about missions. Now, I'm interested in what our church is doing in the world, so I have started to read the information. I even think about people in other places now, like our neighbors to the south, Mexico, and how hard it is for some of them to survive working all day and then to go in to work in other factories and warehouses at night." Through this process, God has opened Cecil's heart and changed his feelings, giving him greater empathy for all citizens of the world. Reflecting on this spiritual transition, Cecil says, "Instead of being an interferer, I want to be a stepping-stone. I have seen the light and I will help in any way I can."

The doors to our church have always been open to whoever wanted to join us, but in the last decade, we have been putting forth a more intentional effort to make it easy for newcomers to find their way to us and to feel at home when they walk in. The realization of the need and the call has led to more open doors in our congregation. This has happened on a large scale in our worship services and on a smaller scale in our classes.

Cecil and his wife helped start a Sunday school class decades ago that is still currently meeting. However, in recent years, as Cecil became aware of what God was doing in the community, our church, and in his heart, he began seeing his ministry in a new light. He said, "I made my amends with God that I would welcome all people like I would want to be welcomed if I went to their country. Now, I like to ask a Korean member of our class to open up our time with prayer in their native tongue—this change in me couldn't have been anything but God."

Many of our international visitors and members are parents who bring their school-aged children along. But as we've seen more international senior adults find their way to us, our older leaders are seeking ways to invite them into the existing programs in the church. Virginia Jones has been excited to see several

Korean members in their seventies begin coming to the senior adult social events, and she hopes that they'll be inviting more friends. She says, "We are hoping to get some of the other cultures to come and join us. The international people I've met here in church are wonderful. I love them and want to get to know them better. Our senior adult social group has a party coming up, and I'm anxious to see how many of our members from African cultures, Asian cultures, and other backgrounds will come to the event." Her hope is for the group to be a place of more mutual sharing of life and culture.

Step Six: Integration

Dr. Michael O. Emerson, provost of North Park University in Chicago, has been tracking multicultural congregations in America since 1998. Emerson defines a congregation as multicultural when at least 20 percent of the attendance represents a people group other than the majority culture. The reasoning behind this is when the 20 percent tipping point is reached, there is a 99 percent probability of random interaction across cultural lines.[10] In other words, the intentional and methodical will become natural and organic.

In 2019, our ministry staff attended the Mosaix Multi-Ethnic Church Conference in Dallas, Texas, where Emerson gave an update on the status of the multicultural church in America. According to the stated definition, 7 percent of evangelical churches were multicultural in 1998. Mark DeYmaz, president and founder of Mosaix Global Network (a multicultural church support group) publicly stated a goal of 20 percent of American churches qualifying to this standard by the year 2020. Emerson was elated to announce that the data in 2019 indicated that 23 percent of evangelical churches qualified as multicultural, accomplishing the goal a year ahead of schedule. At First Baptist Duluth, we crossed this line in 2017. Now, cross-cultural interactions are common, and any cultural barriers are seldom given a second thought. However, it all began with deliberate attempts to recognize people and give opportunities to relate.

I often joke that I moved to Duluth from India, not Indiana. Between my former pastorate in Indianapolis and my current work at First Baptist Duluth, I was a part of a short-term mission trip to India. This endeavor was led by the employees of Lifeway Christian Resources. I was invited to participate as a member of their board of trustees. During my second year in Duluth, I felt the call to return to India and develop a longer-term partnership. Former missionary and legacy member Tom Jones arranged for our team to meet his daughter and son-in-law, who were serving in Delhi at the time. They, in turn, introduced us to Daniel Kumar, pastor of the Good News Centre in New Delhi. During our meeting, I learned that Pastor Daniel has a brother in the United States who lives within a couple miles from our church. Tom Jones and other church members became fast friends with Daniel's brother, Kadmiel, and his family. Later, we will tell the story of their sister, Charlotte, who came from India to do seminary study and serve as a ministry intern on our staff. I have led seven mission teams on trips to India, allowing several of our legacy members to have firsthand experience with one of our key mission partners. Many in our church keep regular contact with Daniel and his ministry in India.

Just after legacy member Lindsay Lapole retired from his job in planned giving with the Salvation Army, he went on one of those mission journeys to India. Lindsay now serves as a member of the Good News Centre board. He raises money and writes grant proposals to get funding from foundations. Lindsay says, "I still don't like Indian food, but I love Indian people. It's been fun working with the Kumars and becoming so connected to their family and ministry. My wife and I have a very close relationship with them. We've gotten to know a lot about the political issues and persecution taking place in India. It's unbelievable to see what those folks are going through today for their faith."

Co-laboring in the church has built a deep friendship. Lindsay Lapole has maintained this connection even after retiring and moving to another state. Recently, when Pastor Daniel Kumar visited Georgia, health issues kept Lindsay from making the long drive back to Duluth for the organization's board meeting. Daniel and Kadmiel Kumar drove more than four hours into the mountains of East Tennessee to Lindsay's new residence. They had dinner with Lindsay and his wife, Bonnie, before driving immediately back to the Atlanta area that same day. In similar fashion, Tom Jones shares the way these cherished friends came through for him: "One of the things that touched me most was when my wife, Nancy, died, and we were at the funeral home visitation before the memorial service. My phone buzzed and it was Daniel Kumar calling all the way from Delhi, India, to express his love and prayer support in my time of grief." First Baptist Duluth has truly become a global community with church family all around the world.

Multicultural transformation was such a challenge for many of our senior adults because of their limited proximity and exposure to people of different backgrounds. We had pockets of diversity in our midst, yes, but many of our members had very little direct interaction with anyone beyond their familiar circle. We had to be intentional to create a safe place of interaction that would promote and foster cross-cultural relationships. Three times a year we host a six-session weekly gathering called "CROSS Class." Each class is comprised of at least three ethnicities and a minimum of thirty-year-age span between the youngest and oldest participants. Therefore, these gatherings genuinely provide a cross-cultural, cross-generational experience. Many lasting friendships develop out of these classes. Through experiences like this, legacy member participants have become great advocates of the church's multicultural vision.

Legacy member Jenny Purcell has lived in Gwinnett County her entire life. She was reared in this church and has never been a member of any other. When she and her husband, Jerry, were asked to be a part of a CROSS Class, they accepted joyfully. Both wanted to meet some of our new international members and support them. One evening, we were discussing the evils of racism when Jenny paused. She went on to share that, as a child, she would never have been allowed to be in the same living room with Black people. When she finished sharing, there was a deafening silence that came over the room. No one knew how to react. All of a sudden, out of the silence, Abioye, our ministry intern from Nigeria, rose from his seat and crossed the room with open arms to give Jenny a hug. That embrace was the teaching moment of the night. Jenny and Jerry sit in the same section of the sanctuary as

Abioye and his family. It is a joy to watch each week as that hug is replayed during the greeting time of the worship service.

Cross-cultural interactions were once strained and awkward at church. Now they are very normal. By intentionally bridging cultural gaps, our legacy members have come to see that people are people. "I sometimes don't even think about where somebody's from anymore, though I do like to know their stories. But we're just used to it," Charles Summerour says. "Our connection group is an outgrowth of CROSS Class, so it's multicultural. We try to invite first-time guests from the previous Sunday's service. We get young people and older people. We are multicultural and multigenerational. When you come to church the next Sunday, you see somebody who already knows who you are."

Cecil Nash has been humbled by the sweet friendship that has developed in his Sunday school class. In his time of need, these newer additions to our church family showed up to be with him, support him, and pray. He says, "Whenever I had the surgery, who was there? Brother Mark was there; and my wife, my daughter, and these two Korean couples from my Sunday school class were there. I have received care and friendship. The people who left our church because of this transition are missing out on the satisfaction I have in knowing the two Korean couples and seeing how much someone different from you can love you."

What happened surrounding Cecil's heart surgery has become a symbol for him of what God is doing in this church. The procedure was fraught with worrisome risks. However, there was the overwhelming support of unexpected friends. There was a coming back to life and the finding of new potential. "If something like that doesn't change your life for the good, then you're hopeless," Cecil says. "I realized I have a new life. My life is like this church. I had to start over. That's what this church is doing in a way. It wasn't dead, but it was in danger of dying, and now it's alive today. Sometimes we don't like lifestyle changes, but we must get used to it and realize that if I'm going to keep living my life, there's changes that have to be made."

Cecil once prided himself on having a tremendous memory. When his health took a turn for the worse, it seemed he wouldn't have the capacity to add new information to that memory bank. But his experience in both his physical and spiritual health has shown that even when a steel trap is rusty and doesn't seem like it will open again, there is still hope. Cecil is creating new technicolor memories. My hope is that these models of transformation can help other churches navigate the tension between old and new. Transitioning churches must proceed with patience, a plan, and consistent follow-through, allowing groups and individuals who once seemed stuck in place to learn and not just tolerate change. This allows legacy members to open up and eventually become the champions of change.

▼ ▼ ▼

CHAPTER THREE

An "Aha" Moment

Stabilization | Appreciation | Multiplication

Now I do all this because of the gospel, so that I
may share in the blessings. (1 Corinthians 9:23)

Many persons have a wrong idea of what constitutes true
happiness. It is not attained through self-gratification but
through fidelity to a worthy purpose. (Helen Keller)

In another part of Georgia, Letty Reeves spent her working years as a schoolteacher and college professor. Then, her husband's Alzheimer's diagnosis changed everything. As his memory and health began to decline, Letty retired from her lifelong work in education to care for him. When her husband died, she wondered: *Here I am, a sixty-two-year-old widow. What am I going to do with the rest of my life?*

As much as most of us prefer for things to stay the same, aging itself implies constant change. No matter how hard we try to secure our lifestyle or relationships, we cannot escape the reality of change! As we age, our health, energy, and physical appearance may go downhill. Our professional roles, family relationships, and friendships may shift. Authors Stuart and Jill Briscoe say, "Aging is inevitable—it's part of being human. And aging means diminishing—it will happen. . . . When we respond to these realities rather than react against them, aging is full of surprises. . . . Humans can and should improve with age. . . ."[11] Second Corinthians 4:16 (NIV) encourages all believers to focus on the unseen as the clock ticks forward: "Therefore we do not lose heart. Though outwardly we are wasting away, yet inwardly we are being renewed day by day." Even as the aging process causes us to diminish outwardly, our spiritual life can undergo unhindered flourishing. The sudden change in Letty's identity and daily activity after her husband's death represented a sad loss but also an amazing time of growth.

After Letty took some time for grief and recovery, a friend in Baton Rouge invited her to Louisiana to teach English to spouses of doctorate students. Letty took her up on the offer and found so much joy in the work that she returned to teach again two summers later. Noticing how she came alive working with students from other nations, friends began to encourage her to take a course called "Perspectives on the Christian World Movement," a curriculum often used to prepare people for the mission field. Letty said when she began to study the material, "It was like a light bulb came on. I thought, 'Where have I been? It's like I've been in some la-la land somewhere.' When I took that course, I vividly realized God's heart for all people. I had known that in my mind, but now I really felt it in my heart. Until then, I had been too involved in living life. But when I took the class, my eyes became totally open to reaching people from all backgrounds for Christ."

God had been doing the same work in our congregation as he had been doing in Letty, even when we did not know one another. After almost a decade of God working in us, we welcomed Letty as a visitor on a Sunday morning. She had just moved to a culturally diverse apartment complex in our community to be closer to her son and grandchild, and she was searching for churches with thriving English programs for internationals. She found First Baptist Duluth and came on her first Sunday in town. God prepared our church for people like Letty and prepared people like Letty for the ministry of our church. By the time Letty came to us, our past struggles created a new strength, leading us into our final steps of the transition process: stabilization, appreciation, and multiplication.

Step Seven: Stabilization

Not everyone will choose to embrace a church's vision to be a place for "all people." When Leland Strange evaluated the early response of the congregation, he estimated 20 percent were enthusiastically in favor of the vision to change our course and attempt to reach our international community effectively. He estimated 20 percent were vehemently against this new direction and opposed almost all attempts to transition the church. That left the vast majority, 60 percent, wondering whether change was necessary and evaluating the viability of the new direction.

This tension among the membership existed for a couple of years. It was a tumultuous time for all of us as many debated the validity of the needs of our city and our calling to address them. Some left our fellowship to settle into congregations that remained more monocultural and, therefore, more comfortable.

Similar to the bereavement process Letty endured as a widow, the existing members who stayed at First Baptist Duluth have experienced loss and grief as friends have left and things have changed around them. Letty had much to grieve. But after a time, she sensed it was right to sell the house and make the move. Likewise, as time went on, legacy church members found themselves less occupied with losses and more focused on opportunities. Like Letty facing her sadness and new identity as a widow, our long-time members emerged from their losses, embraced recovery, and gained a fresh sense of excitement as they explored the possibilities of their changing world and church. This was a big sigh of relief. After a time of so much uncertainty, we were seeing a new stabilization in the fellowship.

Every church attempting to transition to a multicultural model eventually reaches the critical junction where they must move forward with the acknowledgment that old friends have moved on, and old methodologies are no longer able to serve the current reality. The memories remain, but there is a new mission to live out.

Lifeway Research reports that 55 percent of Americans believe that churches are declining, and 42 percent of them believe churches are dying.[12] In many cases, it comes down to choosing between letting go of the former ways of doing things or watching the church fade away altogether. The realization of a church's new reality helps the church, and legacy members in particular, understand and embrace the change necessary to restore or sustain health and become effective in a multicultural community.

When the dust settled, those who remained were increasingly committed to the new work God had for us in our city. And interestingly, we began to notice just how much our new calling matched with the legacy of our church in decades past. Church historian and former deacon chairman Charles Summerour asked, "What would the founders of this church think of the direction that we are taking?" Even beyond our current legacy members, First Baptist Duluth has historically been a church known for acceptance and inclusion. The elementary school across the street from our church bears the name of the late B. B. Harris, father of our current mayor, Nancy Harris. B. B. Harris was a member of First Baptist Duluth and a well-known educator. As superintendent of Gwinnett County Schools during the civil rights era, B. B. Harris led desegregation efforts and even went toe-to-toe with the Ku Klux Klan when they resisted his efforts at justice and racial reconciliation within the community. Mayor Nancy recalls the night that the Klan came and burned a cross in their front lawn. The legacy of this church during the civil rights struggle was now opening the door for a new era for the church with ministries to all nationalities. Charles Summerour concluded that with the legacy of acceptance that had shaped First Baptist Duluth decades ago, our predecessors would view the changes being made as "positive, necessary, and glorifying the Lord."

Most of the congregation did move over time to join the ranks of the early adopters. As Leland points out, "not all were cheerleaders for change." However, Charles Summerour concludes, "Acceptance eventually overcame our differences."

I am humbly grateful for those who acted as liaisons during this critical time of transition. Many showed unwavering support for my leadership and confidence that I was leading under the direction of God's Holy Spirit. Leland quoted Henry Blackaby in an email of affirmation: "When God wants to reveal His will to a church, He will begin by speaking to one or more individuals. Because of the nature of his call and assignment from God, this is often the pastor. . . . The pastor's job is to bear witness to the church about what he senses God is saying." Leland stated that he would support this new direction verbalized by his pastor unless it was derailed by a solid biblical rationale. He would often encourage those contemplating leaving the fellowship to "stick with us and see where God is going to take us." This type of support encouraged other legacy members to warm up to new ideas and opened greater spheres of cooperation.

The stabilization of the church's fellowship directly affects the church's ability to reach financial stability. As numerous neighboring churches began to fade away, key leaders at First Baptist Duluth were analyzing our future viability. Early in our transition process I sought the counsel of successful business leaders in our fellowship. Some had wisely adjusted their own business models in order to thrive in our changing multicultural economy. Leland Strange calls this the "aha moment." People need to arrive at the conclusion that the new direction is in their best interest. That self-realization is often accompanied with financial investment and support.

These critical thinkers aided the church in evaluating our spending practices, the church's staff size and needs, as well as future income potential. This group became the solid financial foundation and continued financial support required for necessary changes to occur. As one leader aptly put it: "This transition was far more than a philosophical change of direction; it was a complete overhaul of how we do ministry." A change of this magnitude needs to be matched by measured financial support. Charles Summerour observed: "This base group offered substantial leadership that provided the opportunity for other legacy members to grow comfortable with the changing environment. Long-tenured members were no longer merely enduring change, but rather embracing it." It is vital that any church seeking to widen the circle of influence get a commitment from the solid members who are undergirding the church's finances. As our members became more unified in their vision, we began to strategize on how to steward the church's shared resources to move forward.

We presented a question that looked to the past—"Do I want to see my past investment in this church come to nothing?"—and members became more engaged in thinking deeply about their role in sustaining the church. Peers sat together over cups of coffee and thought about the one hundred years the church had ministered in that radius, how their parents had brought them to that very church as children, and how God must have a future for it. Leland would say to his friends: "You've invested in the church over the years. Do you personally want to see this church be here or do you want to just leave and watch it disintegrate? Do you have a responsibility not to just go home satisfied every Sunday but to actually contribute? What are you going to do to help it survive as opposed to saying, 'It's all about me'?"

Legacy members were challenged to look to the future: "What is it going to take for us to be here twenty-five or fifty years from now?" This helped our faithful givers to think deeply about their investment in a church that existed within a changing community, understanding that the church will not remain if it does not have its financial security in place. There were some members thinking about leaving the church or staying and blocking the plans or waiting to leave as soon as their child graduated. Yet through the wise counsel of the financial experts in our leadership, many changed their minds, stayed with us, and continued to give.

Our church had experienced a significant reduction in budget giving prior to my arrival. Giving declined more than 60 percent from 2005 to 2010. From 2010 to 2015, the first five years after our transition to a multicultural vision, we experienced a 10-percent increase in budget giving, a significant step in the right direction. Leland says in the five years since then, "If you look at our history of giving, you'll find that it's been almost static (within 5 percent). And yet, many people left. So, who left? It was those who weren't very committed in the beginning, those who weren't invested enough spiritually and relationally to invest financially. Even if they were Sunday school teachers, they really weren't the ones providing the backbone."

We have worked hard to eliminate debt and prioritize giving not only to the church budget, but to exciting ministry

opportunities that help us to better welcome our neighbors into
our church community. We had the unique opportunity to sell
off a large section of our land to bolster our annual budget in the
years to come. That is a great starting point, but it is not a cure-
all. Many churches raise funds for new facilities or renovations.
However, as we moved forward in our new calling, our desire
was to incorporate funding into ministry projects that the general
budget simply could not support. Since no real capital improve-
ments were being attempted on our building, the campaign was
referred to as a "giving initiative" and was aptly named the "One
Fund Campaign," calling attention to our unity in the cause of
Christ. Our members gave $250,000 over and above budget giv-
ing in a two-year time frame to accomplish an array of ministry
projects. These funds provided the impetus for the International
Grounds Café, upgrades to our next-generation ministry areas,
and local ministry projects that put the church on a growing
trajectory. Your church's financial situation may not look exactly
like this. No situation provides a cookie-cutter model for all, but
I hope our experience will give you a few things to consider. Each
church's transformation plan needs to be based on its actual circumstances, challenges, and resources.

Consider your building and the size of your congregation.
Churches that have declined significantly in attendance may
struggle to pay for utilities or repairs, especially high-ticket items
like a new roof or parking lot. We have a large building that was
bustling with activity in the '80s and '90s, but the cost of operating a building our size could overwhelm a congregation if its
attendance and giving were to decline significantly.

Consider the cultural background of your growing international church. Do your newcomers have a history in churches that teach financial giving, or do they have a history resembling more centralized churches in which the local congregation doesn't directly fund the care of the building or the salaries of the clergy? Or is it possible that they do not have a history in church and stewardship at all. Newcomers from a centralized church background or unchurched background may need more time and discipleship to understand their individual role in contributing to the financial health of the church to ensure future sustainability. Effective stewardship education will teach new members the importance of financial stability and invite them into the joy of giving, modeled by the generosity and commitment of the legacy members.

This is God's church, and He has made us the managers of it. Without the solid foundation of our existing givers, our church could not have sustained this transition. On top of a solid biblical foundation, every new work, whether a church plant or the transition of an existing church, needs to have a stable financial plan. Our call was to invite our neighbors to join our fellowship, hoping they would come to call our church their church home, too. That kind of hospitality requires an investment of resources to prepare the place and the programs, and to gather materials to share with a broader community. A church cannot keep its lights on or its ministries flourishing without the investment of the people within its pews. Once giving declines, losses can snowball. It is important to communicate the vital need for stable giving early on in the church's transition. It is vital to develop a team mentality among the existing members so that the church can maintain the resources to fulfill its purpose. This strong base of giving among long-time church members can then provide a good model for newcomers who may not have been discipled in the importance of stewardship. The new work God has been doing in this congregation has been spurred on by the giving of our faithful legacy members.

Step Eight: Appreciation

Since 2017, 60 percent of the new members at First Baptist Duluth have been people of color. This incredible growth in diversity has created cross-cultural interactions that have changed the dynamics of our congregation forever. I have told numerous peers and colleagues that, having experienced the joys of pastoring a wonderfully diverse congregation, I cannot imagine ever being part of a church that does not openly reflect all the people of its community. Immersion in a diverse community will tend to cause one of two reactions: seclusion into circles of homogeneity, or inclusion, leading to cultural discovery and profound appreciation. Unfortunately, the former reaction has been the American church default for the past generation. The explosion of diversity in the metro areas of our country has exposed the poor practices of many congregations that are theologically flawed and potentially racist.

At First Baptist Duluth, we chose the path of inclusion, and it has led even once-resistant members to a newfound appreciation of diversity. As the church membership has diversified, meaningful cross-cultural relationships have enlightened legacy members to strengths that are brought to the church from the cultural richness of our new members. One such strength is the incredible attention to prayer that is prevalent among Korean churches. Many Korean congregations in our area open their church buildings at 5:00 a.m. every morning for a prayer gathering to start the day. As Korean families have tasted the culture of the American church, many have been surprised by the lack of a significant prayer emphasis.

Former Deacon Chairman Charles Summerour observed that although the Korean commitment to the priority of prayer was far superior to our church's efforts, not once did he hear an attitude of superiority or spiritual arrogance. To the contrary, Charles recalled when Dr. KJ Lee, a Korean research doctor, came to First Baptist Duluth, KJ would attend the traditional Wednesday night prayer meeting that had been held at the church for years. This meeting had dropped off to a small number of older members who prayed mainly for one another and their peers, predominantly for health concerns. Summerour noted that this new Korean member attended and quietly participated during some of these prayer sessions, though we would later learn of the dynamic prayer ministry he had experienced back in his native country. KJ has proven himself to be a genuine servant leader. Later, he was elected to serve as a deacon in the church. At the time of this writing, he has been elected to serve as the chairman of the deacon body and is leading the deacons and the entire church into an increased emphasis on prayer. Currently, he leads a dynamic Saturday morning prayer effort that is changing the spiritual temperature of the entire church.

Another type of cultural nuance that has added significantly to the effectiveness of First Baptist Duluth is the demonstrative worship style prevalent among our African members. Currently, people from ten different African countries have become a part of our church family. Although each nation has their own language, foods, and cultural traditions, they all express themselves in dance and worship styles that stretch our congregation to experience something far beyond our traditions. Legacy member Virginia Jones describes how she feels about the music and expressive worship of our African friends: "There has been a noticeable change in our church's music. Many African choir members are very animated in worship. They move a lot. We [legacy members] are kind of stodgy sometimes. The new music at First Baptist Duluth is wonderful." One of the church's longest-tenured members, Wilbur Brooks, thinks that the addition of our African brothers and sisters has aided him in loosening inhibitions in worship: "When I watch the African people dance and sing, it helps to open up this reserved Southern-born child."

Another example of beneficial cross-cultural exchange has been the profound respect that our Asian members hold for the elders of their culture. During our East Asian New Year service, there is a time set aside for the children of the church to give gifts to anyone present who is over the age of eighty. This practice has taught us the cultural value that is placed on the eldest generation by our Asian friends, but it has also endeared the international community to the legacy members of our congregation. As recipients of a special gift in this traditional celebration, many senior members of the church now have beautiful framed artwork on their walls, reminders of honor and friendship shown by the Asian members of the fellowship. Some legacy members have even questioned why people from American culture are not equally respectful of our elder generation. These and other examples of cultural exchange have led to an honest appreciation for others' cultural upbringing.

The interesting thing about the big changes in our church is that those who stayed, even those who were resistant to leaving our monocultural ways behind, have come to appreciate the uniqueness of our diverse congregation. Lindsay Lapole and his wife moved to Tennessee not too long ago and began attending a church that is monocultural and traditional, similar to the way First Baptist Duluth used to do church a decade ago. Lindsay says, "Now, we miss the variety in the worship service. Even though I was never all that excited about singing in all the different languages, when you're not around it anymore, you miss it. You miss seeing all the people in their different native attire. You miss saying hello, speaking, interacting, and knowing about others' lives here and back where they came from. You miss the international feel. And I think there is a spirit of openness and fun and joy that was in Duluth that is missing where we are now. Here, you never see the dancing. You never see the celebration. You never see the many different people. We have come to appreciate First Baptist Duluth a whole lot more since we left it. It's the atmosphere that's been built there. We miss it."

This new way of worship and fellowship, now appreciated by our long-time members, has made our church more attractive to others who are from the same generation but who would not have been drawn to the church in its less-diverse form. Letty Reeves says of her first visit to our service, "I just loved it—the church was truly culturally diverse! There were Americans, Chinese, Korean, Japanese, Africans. It was great! And we were all worshiping the Lord!" She visited two or three other churches and found that the congregations were mostly White. People from international origin were provided a separate service at a different time or in an alternate place, but these churches failed to provide an integrated cultural community of faith. She thought, "No, that is not the kind of church I'm looking for. If I want to go to church with just White people, I can move back to my old town where I already know everybody, and I don't have to make any new friends." She quickly returned to us at First Baptist Duluth. She went to Sunday school, and again she found that the classes were culturally diverse. She tried a First Connections group and it, too, was multicultural. There were people of all ages and ethnicities and language backgrounds just having a meal, talking, and enjoying the life of faith together. What she saw at church on Sunday was what she saw in the group on Monday and throughout every aspect of the fellowship. We were the diverse congregation that Letty was looking for. We are a vibrant multicultural church that our legacy members may not have been looking for, but have now learned to appreciate fully.

Step Nine: Multiplication

There is a reward for remaining faithful on this technicolor journey. The apostle Paul concluded the reasoning for his willingness to become "all things to all people" (1 Cor. 9:22), saying, "Now I do all this because of the gospel, so that I may share in the blessings" (v. 23). God will honor these efforts. The technicolor path is perilous, filled with opposition, misunderstandings, and relational hazards. However, the reward of the technicolor path is priceless. It has been a blessing to observe God gathering like-minded people with a shared passion to lead this effort.

Our legacy members already exhibited a natural hospitality that made our church an inviting place, but as they stretched themselves to relate with people from very different backgrounds and test their Southern charm in new contexts, their hospitality became much more than good manners, a smile, and a hearty handshake, or inviting familiar friends over for a good meal. In this new adventure, their hospitality has taken on biblical, Spirit-filled dimensions.

Biblical hospitality goes beyond entertaining those in our inner circle. It finds us pulling up a chair to sit with the unfamiliar. The Greek word for *hospitality* used throughout the New Testament is *philoxenos/philoxenia*, which literally means "love toward the stranger," especially people from other nations, languages, and ethnicities. Real hospitality crosses dividing lines and makes it possible for people who were once strangers to become like family.

Hebrews 13:1–2 (NIV) says: "Keep on loving one another as brothers and sisters. Do not forget to show hospitality to strangers, for by so doing some people have shown hospitality to angels without knowing it." Our existing relationships with close friends and long-time church members are of great value and should continue to be nurtured, but Scripture tells us that in the comfort of our existing community, we should be careful not to turn inward. Healthy community is not stagnant; it is growing, turned outward, always seeking to invite and include and expand its reach.

As our members have pulled up more seats to the table and widened our circle, our capacity for hospitality has multiplied.

Members have learned to practice hospitality in new ways to create an environment that is more inviting to those from diverse minority backgrounds. At the same time, God has been gathering people from the majority culture who are themselves on a journey of discovery. Many are in search of opportunities to participate in a meaningful multicultural community of faith. This includes people like our friend Letty, as well as younger families whose worldview has expanded in recent years.

Steve and Julie Higgins attended a large church in a very diverse city in Louisiana. Their kids attended a magnet school there, and when their son had his graduation party, two-thirds of the classmates that came to the party were from different ethnic backgrounds. Over time, the Higginses' sons began to challenge the parents about the lack of diversity in their circles, asking, "Who do you have in your life who's not like you?" The Higginses slowly became more aware of the company they were keeping in life and ministry. Reflecting on their time in Louisiana, Steve says, "We had a wonderful pastor, church, and ministries, but what became striking to me was that when I went to church, pretty much everybody looked just like me. Something did not sit right with me about that. Why does it look different inside the walls of the church than it does outside the walls of the church? We moved to Duluth with our questions about diversity and the church percolating in the background." While God was nudging Steve and Julie out from their status quo, God was nudging First Baptist Duluth out from ours.

God was preparing the Higgins family for a new way of life and service and was preparing our church to be a place to equip and encourage people with that kind of vision and passion. When

Steve retired from the Air Force, he took a new job as chief medical officer at a hospital in our county. The Higgins family visited different places around the community and were blown away by the diversity. "God was working on my heart. I saw this as a need. I prayed that God would lead us to the right church to allow us to experience the richness of the diversity of cultures within the community where we live and work. This church is the place God was preparing us for."

In their Sunday school class, Steve and Julie study alongside a woman from China, a couple from Burma, a couple from Ethiopia, a couple from Taiwan, and another White couple. The class is led by a research doctor from India. "It's the neatest thing being able to interact, hear different perspectives, and have fellowship with people from so many different cultures," says Steve. Yet, the benefit goes beyond time spent on Sunday mornings.

Steve and Julie enjoy serving on the leadership team of the First Connections ministry. First Connections meets every other week for the purpose of welcoming first-time visitors to the church and connecting them to the fellowship by hosting them in a host home for a "get to know us" dinner party. On one occasion Steve and Julie reported having thirty people from eleven different nations present in their home for a dinner party! These groups informally discuss the previous Sunday's sermon and attempt to provide avenues for new people to find meaningful connections to the church body. Steve recalls that one week when the previous week's sermon was about being a good neighbor, they hosted dinner guests from Taiwan, Ghana, and Nigeria, and some Muslim friends as well. What a great way to put the sermon into practice!

The practice of hospitality in our congregation gives each of our members greater confidence and capacity to interact with the diverse neighbors they see in their workplaces, housing divisions, or local retail establishments. Julie says that in our congregation, her close friendships with two Indian women, Charlotte and Ruth, have made it easier for her to make South Asian friends out in the community. Julie and Charlotte have enjoyed extending hospitality beyond the doors of the church as they spend time with an unchurched friend from Bangladesh that Julie met at a local ministry thrift store. "It enriches our lives. It opens our eyes to the world and makes it easier to share the gospel with people from other countries," Julie says. "And with Charlotte, I feel like I have a friend and a teammate who understands cultures that are foreign to me and can help me share with people from her part of the world in a culturally appropriate way." As we have incorporated international celebrations into the life of our church, Steve has also found himself feeling more familiar with different cultures and better able to connect in his daily comings and goings. "Now that I have a little more familiarity with Indian culture, I'm able to engage with the Indian couple at our local dry cleaners. There is a greater comfort, and I can have conversations about Indian Independence Day and break the ice with the fact that we celebrate that holiday at our church. This gives me a chance to invite them to take part."

The partnership between those from American culture and those from international backgrounds has greatly multiplied our effectiveness in ministry. Similarly, God has provided connections that allow Letty Reeves to use her old skills and gifts in a new way, expanding her capacity to serve in her retirement. After

Letty joined the church, she became a teacher in our English as a Second Language (ESL) program. This allowed her to use her educational background and love for teaching in this new phase of life. She has developed beautiful friendships through that outreach effort and in the congregation on Sundays. Currently, she is building relationships, seeking to become a real friend, not just to see someone at church. Sometimes, she even goes with a student to a Chinese market to get to know her world. Other times, she takes a student to lunch and they laugh as they both fight to pay for the bill.

Within our congregation, Letty, too, has connected with Charlotte Kumar. Though they come from two different cultures, they have many interests in common. Charlotte moved from India to the United States to pursue her doctorate in ministry and serve as a ministry intern on our staff. Her doctorate writing project was to develop a curriculum to train church members in how to witness to their Hindu neighbors. Letty has a doctorate in education and has worked extensively in the area of curriculum development. A natural friendship developed when Charlotte asked Letty to proofread her dissertation. Letty had the experience, enthusiasm, and time to help. Soon, they began collaborating on Charlotte's curriculum project. Letty said, "God has given me a lot of opportunities to be involved with internationals. That is where my heart is. That is what I wanted to do all along, but I had to find the place that would encourage me and provide the tools. Now I get to be a missionary and I don't even have to go overseas. I get to be involved in people's lives. It is like a whole new life for me. It's a whole new world God has brought me into. I've made some dear friends and it's given meaning and purpose to my life."

God is providing an obvious blessing by bringing like-minded people to this extraordinary multicultural work. But more importantly, God is blessing us and others by bringing members of the international community to faith in Christ! Even the legacy members who were once skeptical about the changes are now taking note of life-changing salvation decisions. Lindsay Lapole joyfully reports, "We baptized seven people last Easter Sunday. I have wondered how many churches in this country baptized seven people on an Easter Sunday morning. We see families being added to the church almost every week. People are beginning to say, 'Okay, whatever's going on here is good.' Whatever is going on here is making it comfortable for people from different backgrounds to respond to the gospel, and that is really the goal."

Legacy members have experienced the blessing of new members who have a shared vision for multicultural work joining the ranks and immediately becoming involved in the work. They have also seen God's hand in reaching people from a variety of different backgrounds and cultural origins. The technicolor process is coming full circle as legacy members have seen their own peers participating in a ministry that multiplies. The path began with observation. However, the path does not end with multiplication. It merely begins a new generation of path-followers who are traveling the beautiful journey to technicolor ministry. Many legacy members have expressed the sense of joy in bringing a friend or neighbor to introduce them to the extraordinary work of First Baptist Duluth and proudly watching them embrace the tenets of multicultural ministry.

Our legacy members have obeyed God's call to love their neighbors, including those who do not look or talk like they do. Their passion for living out the Great Commission has been reignited in our church and in their daily comings and goings. Their cooperation has been fruitful. They have stretched themselves and seen tremendous growth that goes beyond their own personal efforts—the kind of growth that equips believers to minister and see God move in a remarkable way in the surrounding community.

SECTION TWO

Languages

Immigration | Immersion | Isolation

Accommodation | Consideration | Acculturation

Redemption | Dedication | Commission

▼ ▼ ▼

CHAPTER FOUR

Jesus Was an Immigrant

Immigration / Immersion / Isolation

*From one man he has made every nationality to
live over the whole earth and has determined their
appointed times and the boundaries of where they
live. He did this so that they might seek God, and
perhaps they might reach out and find him, though
he is not far from each one of us.* (Acts 17:26–27)

*Into every culture, God puts glimpses of grace
to capture people's attention and prepare them
to hear the message of Christ.* (Zig Ziglar)

Every person who calls America home is either an immigrant or
the descendant of immigrants, with, of course, the exception
of Native Americans. *Webster's Dictionary* defines *immigrant* as,
"a person who comes to a country to take up residence." A *refugee*

is "a person who flees to a foreign country to escape persecution or danger." These words are not interchangeable, although
they are often used as such. As of 2020, the United States has
opened the door to approximately one million immigrants each
year. However, of those one million immigrants who arrive on
American soil annually, only 85,000 refugees are allowed to enter.
These are the difficult stories of those fleeing persecution, war,
famine, totalitarian governments, and even threats of death.

Most Christians have never considered that Jesus was both an
immigrant and a refugee. He claimed in John 6:38: "I have come
down from heaven, not to do my own will, but the will of him
who sent me." He left His home in heaven to take new residence
in a distant land when He came to earth, making Him an immigrant. Jesus was also a refugee. In Matthew's account of the birth
of Jesus, the Gospel is careful to note that Mary and Joseph fled
with Jesus to Egypt because "Herod is about to search for the
child to kill him" (Matt. 2:13). Therefore, Jesus knows firsthand
the hardships, challenges, needs, and hopes of immigrants and
refugees. Much of His earthly teaching can be couched in the
context of how believers should respond to the needs of immigrants and refugees. A 2015 study conducted by Lifeway Research
revealed that only 12 percent of evangelical Christians get their
view of immigration from the Bible. Unfortunately, rather than
leaning on Scripture, the vast majority of American believers are
forming their views of immigrants based on information ascer-
tained from Fox News, CNN, the *Wall Street Journal*, and the
Washington Post.

Jesus taught about the day of reckoning at the end of time in
Matthew 25:31–46. He said that "all the nations will be gathered

before him" (v. 32). The word *nations* is derived from the word *ethnos,* meaning ethnicities. There are no exclusions. Every ethnicity will stand before Him. And although there are hundreds of ethnicities, Jesus will divide people into two categories in the same way that a shepherd would separate the sheep from the goats within his herd (vv. 32–34). Jesus went on to give the most explicit instructions for how believers should treat the immigrants among us. He said:

> "I was hungry and you gave me something to eat; I was thirsty and you gave me something to drink; I was a stranger and you took me in; I was naked and you clothed me; I was sick and you took care of me; I was in prison and you visited me." (vv. 35–36)

The listeners were puzzled as to when they had ever shown these tangible displays of compassion for Jesus, which they were now being commended for. Jesus explained, "'Truly I tell you, whatever you did for one of the least of these brothers and sisters of mine, you did for me'" (v. 40).

God is bringing the nations to this country. He is going to hold us accountable for whether we seize or squander this opportunity to make a positive impact on the world. I have observed the explosion of migration in the metro Atlanta area since my arrival in 2010. According to the *Atlanta Journal Constitution,* for eight consecutive years, from 2010 to 2017, Atlanta was the number-one destination for those seeking a new place of residence in the United States. The city slipped to third in 2018, surpassed only by Washington, DC, and Dallas. As a close northern suburb of the city, our area has exploded in growth, making our county school system the largest in the state of Georgia. The migration to our area has offered a colorful change to the demographic landscape of Duluth.

Southern Baptists have been identified as outstanding proponents of missionary efforts to carry the gospel to the "uttermost part of the earth" (Acts 1:8 KJV). However, the nations are now our neighbors, and it remains to be seen how churches will respond. Former International Mission Board President Dr. David Platt coined a phrase, "missionally malignant." Platt defines this as a "willingness to go around the world to reach an unreached people group yet ignore the same people group as one's next-door neighbor." While attending a conference on reaching the nations, I heard Southeastern Baptist Theological Seminary President Dr. Daniel Akin state that "60 percent of immigrants in America do not know one single Christian." This is an indictment upon the church in America.

In section 1 of this book, I spoke about the mindset shift that was necessary among the "legacy members," long-tenured people within the congregation. In this section, I want to share the stories of the "language members" of our church. These first- and second-generation immigrants also had to pass through a change in mindset in order to participate in a multicultural church. Many had to leave the comforts of their own language group to become a team member in something bigger than their own culture. The following is their path into technicolor ministry.

Step One: Immigration

We conducted more than a dozen interviews of immigrants and refugees affiliated with First Baptist Duluth. Their stories of immigration are as unique as their thumbprints. And yet, each had a burning desire to adopt a new homeland.

David came from Afghanistan as a political refugee. Mae and Li have similar stories as Chinese housewives who came to America with their businessmen husbands, but both said the attraction to Duluth was the existing Chinese population and good Chinese grocery stores. Jeffrey was reared as a Buddhist in Indonesia. After he became a Christian, he planned to come to the United States and attend a Christian college. Joseph and Youngmi were serving as Korean nonprofit workers in the impoverished nation of Nepal, when they sensed a calling to come to the United States, study English, and plan for a lifetime of Christian mission work. Paola was a teenager living in Mexico City, when her father told the family that they would uproot and move to America to attend Bible college and start a Spanish-speaking church. Edith was left behind with extended family in Mexico by a mother who moved to America to make a new life, promising to retrieve her children at the first possible opportunity. Victoria and Kayode were fortunate winners of a visa lottery in Nigeria that enabled them to move here in search of a better life for their children. Halimeh moved from Iran to escape the economic collapse that happened in her country after the revolution.

These stories are rich with passion, littered with heartaches, and filled with challenges that the average American-born person cannot begin to comprehend. However, the one common thread that runs through these testimonies is the incredible sovereignty of God!

Nowhere is that truer than in the story of a Korean couple, Sung-gil Hong (Gilbert) and Se-jung Hwang (Lucy). Prior to coming to the United States, Gilbert and Lucy lived in Nepal, where Gilbert served at the Korean Embassy for six years. Both of them came from Christian families in Korea. Lucy was reared in a Methodist church and Gilbert in a Presbyterian one. However, as they began life together as a married couple, Lucy became concerned about Gilbert's lackadaisical commitment to his faith. While serving in Nepal, the Hongs became close friends with a Korean missionary couple.

Gilbert desired to move from his diplomatic post in Nepal to a more developed country, so he requested a transfer. Shortly thereafter, the couple learned that their new place of service would be in the United States at the Korean Embassy in Atlanta. Excited about their upcoming move, Gilbert and Lucy shared the news with their missionary cohorts. Their missionary friends had known of Lucy's concern about Gilbert's faith, and they immediately recommended a strong Korean congregation that they felt confident would disciple the Hongs and answer any questions that Gilbert might be facing. Lucy said that she was claiming the promise of Romans 10:17: "So faith comes from what is heard, and what is heard comes through the message about Christ." The missionaries considered the pastor of the recommended church to be one of the most outstanding communicators they knew and a champion for proclaiming truth.

When the Hongs arrived in the United States, Lucy immediately began to petition Gilbert that they attend the recommended church. However, Gilbert expressed a desire to attend a "local church." Serving as a diplomat at the Korean Consulate, Gilbert felt a step outside of his Korean culture would be a break from work and a welcome respite on the weekends. Reluctantly, Lucy began a search for an American church where they could become involved. Lucy fervently prayed that this decision would be a far deeper investment than merely a perfunctory place for them to meet people on Sundays. Her search eventually led her to our congregation. She learned that this American church had Korean staff members, offered language interpretation services in Korean, and even sponsored a Korean culture school that was embracing the rapidly growing Korean population in the area.

Gilbert and Lucy were immediately impressed by the receptivity of our congregation and made friends quickly. One of the first families to befriend the Hongs was the Kim family. Dr. Joseph and Youngmi Kim had also served in Nepal before coming to the United States. Joseph had accepted an appointment for international service after graduating from medical school in Korea, similar in scope to the work of the United States Peace Corp. The Kims were now in the United States to become immersed in English as Joseph did seminary studies in preparation for missionary service. The Kims were also good friends with the missionary mentors of Gilbert and Lucy from their days in Nepal. In summary, a Korean missionary couple in Nepal had sent Gilbert and Lucy to the United States recommending a specific Korean church to aid them in their spiritual pilgrimage. When Gilbert rejected that plan, God led the couple to First Baptist Duluth, where they would meet another Korean couple that had also moved from Nepal and were preparing for missionary service. God's sovereignty in this incredible act was an overwhelming confirmation to Gilbert and Lucy that they were in the exact place God wanted them to be.

Lucy said that upon beginning to attend First Baptist Duluth, she prayed fervently for God to make His will known to their family. One night when she was praying, she heard the voice of God: "Lucy, is it the work of the shepherd or the sheep to find pasture and clean water for the flock?" Lucy acquiesced, "Lord, it is Your job and not mine." Lucy said from that epiphany forward, she never worried about whether they had made the right decision in coming to our congregation. Soon, the two of them became involved in a variety of ministries and activities around the church. Gilbert served as an interpreter on Sunday mornings. Lucy became active in women's Bible studies and served in the weekday preschool ministry. Both of them volunteered for the food distribution ministry.

My first interaction with this precious couple was at a Christmas luncheon that we hosted in our home for the Korean members of our church. Gilbert and Lucy were invited by numerous Korean members to come and meet the pastor and his wife. On that occasion, I learned that Gilbert was struggling with his job at the consulate. He wanted to resign his position, but doing so would revoke his diplomatic visa status and mean that he and Lucy would be required to return to Korea. This dilemma provided numerous opportunities over the coming months to have meaningful conversations with Gilbert about his future and God's plan for his life.

Gilbert and Lucy attended a CROSS Class in our home. This gathering consists of six weekly meetings with the agenda being to learn and appreciate people from a variety of different cultural perspectives. Typically, these cultural laboratories are comprised of about twenty to twenty-five people from ten to twelve different nationalities. Being a trained diplomat, Gilbert was enamored with the church's concerted efforts to bring diverse ethnicities together in a harmonious effort. Lucy described one of the very first services that she and Gilbert attended at First Baptist Duluth: "At the conclusion of the service, we sang 'Make Us One.' This simple melody was new to me, but I recognized its scriptural basis (John 13:34–35). . . . I found myself singing this new praise song throughout my week. I was consistently reminding myself of the truth that people will recognize our discipleship when we unite and love one another." Gilbert and Lucy were no longer viewing the multicultural blend of our church as an outreach strategy, but as the honest pursuit of the will of God for ministry in our setting. They explained, "When we go to the Father's House (heaven), I am sure that it will look very much like the multicultural church."

Despite being active in every area of the church's ministry, the Hongs had not become official members of the congregation. They often used the excuse of their tentative position with the consulate as the reasoning for their lack of a decision about church membership. Gilbert's displeasure with his role was increasing and causing great angst about their future. On a Sunday after church, Gilbert informed me that he had resigned his post and that he and Lucy had a short time to request a different visa status or they would be asked to return to Korea. Lucy was devastated by these circumstances. She had made numerous lifelong friends in the congregation. Gilbert, however, was much more reserved and spent time examining their options. They first shared this confidential information with Dr. Joseph and Youngmi Kim. At this time, Joseph had been selected and ordained as one of the deacons of the church. He and Youngmi were viewed as strong spiritual advisers who could offer tremendous insight. Joseph challenged Gilbert that the real issue was not his employment or their visa status. God was trying to get his attention to make the spiritual decision that had been on his heart since his days in Nepal. Gilbert accepted the gentle rebuke from his best friend and asked how he could experience the peace of God. Joseph then led him into a relationship with Jesus Christ. Gilbert called me shortly thereafter and asked if he and Lucy could make an appointment to see me and discuss believer's baptism and church membership.

In January of 2020, I had the wonderful privilege of baptizing the Hongs as members of our church family. Lucy stated, "This baptism was a spiritual mark for both of us that we are serious about our commitment to Christ. It was a renewal of our marriage and the beginning of our shared life in Christ." The Hongs have faced a number of challenges since their baptism, including relocating to Korea. On their first Saturday back in their native country, they joined our Zoom prayer meeting that gathers at 7:00 a.m. each weekend. On the next day, they were present via Zoom in their young adult Bible study group and present on the live-streaming worship experience. This incredible couple may no longer be physically present at our church meetings, but they have had a spiritual encounter that has changed the direction of their lives. God is orchestrating connections across national boundaries that not only affect the physical and emotional well-being of immigrants, but also contribute to their spiritual growth and salvation. What a privilege to bear witness to God's redemptive plan! His power is not limited by geographical boundaries, language limitations, or cultural differences.

Step Two: Immersion

Jeffrey Go's testimony of rapid immersion into American culture helps our church to better understand the challenging path that many immigrants take to get to us and just how much change they've experienced. Jeffrey was born in Indonesia and is the son of Chinese Buddhist parents. He attended a Buddhist elementary school through the fourth grade at the behest of his parents. The family moved within Indonesia that year and enrolled Jeffrey in a Catholic school in their new community. This was his first introduction to Christianity as a religion. By his high school years, his parents agreed to send him to a private Christian school. There, he would be exposed to Bible lessons and chapel services, and be surrounded by friends who were followers of Jesus. Jeffrey recalls the invitations that came from his new peers to attend Sunday services, Bible studies, and youth retreats. It was on one of those youth retreats that Jeffrey became a Christian and began his walk with the Lord. Indonesia is the largest Muslim country in the world, and his parents are Chinese Buddhist. As Jeffrey gave his life to Christ, he was a minority among minorities: a Chinese-Indonesian and a former Buddhist in a Muslim nation who was now a believer in the Lord Jesus Christ.

After graduating high school, Jeffrey received the opportunity to come to the United States and study at Pensacola

Christian College. His parents were extremely supportive of this open door and encouraged him to pursue it with diligence. The thirteen-hour transcontinental flight to the States was his first time ever leaving Indonesia. Jeffrey expected that his biggest challenge would be improving his English skills. Jeffrey recalls that although he was anxious and possibly a little scared, he was incredibly excited at the prospect of what God was going to do in this new phase of his life.

Upon arrival in Florida, culture shock began to set in. Absolutely nothing was the same as "back home." Americans drove on the "wrong" side of the road, they ate the strangest things, and his two new college roommates, both White, carried on the most unusual conversations. Jeffrey found himself completely immersed in a new culture and had no handles to grasp and steady himself. His four-year degree in marketing would yield far more than an education in principles of human behavior and finance. This time would be a total rearrangement of his worldview and a radical readjustment to his definition of "normal."

Jeffrey attempted to involve himself in numerous campus groups to aid in his acclimation to his new homeland. One of his favorite extracurricular activities was his involvement in the campus choir. During the rehearsals, a pretty girl caught his attention. He learned through a mutual friend that the girl's name was Anna. An awkward attempt to get the two of them together at a group dinner imploded when Anna did not show up due to a conflict she was having with a roommate. On the day before graduation, the choir was practicing for the next day's exercises, and they at last exchanged phone numbers. Anna and Jeffrey were both graduating. Anna was staying on campus as she looked for employment, and Jeffrey had to complete some coursework post-graduation. They found themselves among the last remaining students on a mostly deserted campus.

Their job search and budding romance would eventually relocate them to metro Atlanta, where Anna became an office administrator for a surgeon and Jeffrey would manage a Chick-fil-A restaurant. The two married and began attending a mega-church in the area. In 2018, Jeffrey made a trip back to Indonesia to aid his parents in making a move. Anna's parents, first-generation immigrants from Korea, came from Wisconsin to stay with their daughter during her husband's absence. During their stay, a Chinese neighbor of Anna's invited them to an event at First Baptist Duluth as we were celebrating East Asian New Year. Over half the world celebrates the New Year on the lunar calendar rather than the solar calendar. Therefore, the large population of East Asians in our area celebrate the New Year somewhere between late January and mid-February. Anna thought that her parents would possibly enjoy this recognition of their culture far more than attending her typical worship service.

Anna was amazed at the cross-cultural experience at First Baptist Duluth. She noticed the more than forty flags from different countries in the sanctuary. She saw the bulletins offered in Korean, Spanish, and Mandarin, and she observed the church service celebrating the lunar new year with a performance by a Korean fan dance team. Anna's mom wondered aloud if this might be the place for Anna and Jeffrey to worship and become invested as a young, cross-cultural couple. When Jeffrey returned from Indonesia, Anna shared with him the delightful experience at our church. They began attending together, and Jeffrey was impressed with how quickly the congregation became like family.

Jeffrey had jumped into the deep end of the pool and was now completely immersed, not only in his new home but in a vibrant, cross-cultural faith community. In only a few short years, Jeffrey had gone from a Chinese Buddhist upbringing in a predominantly Muslim country to becoming a believer in Christ, being a graduate of a Christian college, marrying a wonderful Christian lady, and becoming actively involved in a dynamic multicultural American church. His story represents so many others like him who have been immersed in a totally new environment.

Once immigrants arrive in the United States, the challenges begin to mount quickly. Our church has made extraordinary steps to address the most significant of these hurdles. Many newcomers lack sufficient English skills to perform even the most rudimentary functions of everyday life in this country. We take great pride in having one of the largest English as a Second Language (ESL) schools in our county. These classes are offered weekly at no cost. Along with English instruction, we offer a life skills component that helps students with driving etiquette, American customs, and colloquialisms. The simple act of enrolling children in public schools is an example of a major obstacle for a new family that lacks proficient English. At the end of class, we offer a Bible reading club that gives students a profound spiritual dimension to their lesson. Mentoring and personal discipleship play key roles in this ministry.

Jesus wanted to meet the physical needs of the immigrant (Matt. 25:31–46) in order to have a hearing to meet their spiritual needs. We are here to aid our immigrant friends in their

JESUS WAS AN IMMIGRANT   103

adjustments to life within a new context. The major changes taking place in their surroundings create great opportunities for gospel conversations.

Step Three: Isolation

Many of our immigrant friends arrived in the United States with big dreams but few possessions. One family shared how they lived in a car for the first six months of their time in America. Most American-born citizens have no idea of the hardships faced by the typical immigrant family in making America their home. Unfortunately, the political debates that have taken place regarding the issues of immigration have greatly dehumanized the process and exasperated the problems that remain in our flawed system.

Lucy Hwang observed that Duluth is one of the most diverse places she has ever lived. It is easy to spot the people who obviously come from a different culture or speak a different language than yourself. However, until she came to our church, Lucy felt that the diverse citizens of Duluth might "share the same space," but they were not "sharing each other's lives." The predicted demographic movement of people is that those who share the same culture, the same language, and the same values will tend to congregate together. But without these lines crossing, how can those with little experience and resources be expected to make it in their adopted homeland?

I have observed how the feeling of isolation is overwhelming to newcomer families in America. In 2017, our church helped Nigerian pastor Abioye Tela and his wife, Joke (pronounced

Joe-Kay), and their children, Aanu and Anjola, move to the United
States so that Pastor Abioye could begin his doctoral degree. As
we prepared for their arrival, our church searched for a living
arrangement that would meet the young family's needs. I heard
of a neighboring church that had a vacant parsonage they were
no longer using that could possibly be rented. As is the case with
most church-owned property, the house was immediately adjacent
to the church that owned it. I took one of our deacons, Babatunde
Adewoye, with me to tour the home. Babatunde and his family
had immigrated from Nigeria just a few years earlier. I felt certain that Babatunde could help me in understanding the needs
of a newly immigrated family. As we walked through the house,
Babatunde commented on its spacious rooms, and I thought that
he was pleased with the potential arrangement. Upon completion
of our tour, Babatunde and I drove back to our church. As soon
as we pulled out of sight of the brick home, my deacon adviser
surrendered his opinion: "This will not work." I inquisitively pro-
tested: "What's wrong with the house? The price, the space, the
availability—all meet our pressing needs." Babatunde responded,
"Not enough neighbors! When Nigerians arrive in America,
they can adapt quickly. However, they are dependent upon the
kindness of their neighbors to aid them through the transition
period." This cultural learning experience has had a profound
effect on ministry decisions that have followed. Our church opted
to locate Pastor Abioye and his family in an apartment complex
much closer to our church campus, where they would have plenty
of neighbors and church members available to ease their isolation
and make their transition a smooth one.

One Friday, I was working alone in the church office when I observed a family driving in circles around the church parking lot. My curiosity was raised when I saw a man and woman get out of their vehicle and take pictures of the church building. I went to the door, invited the visitors to come in, and learned that the woman was enrolled in an architecture class at a local community college. One of her assignments was to take photographs of varied architectural styles within the community. I invited them inside the church building to get a closer look at the facility. This was my first encounter with Victoria and Kayode Ajai. When I learned that they were from Nigeria, I told them about our ministry intern, Abioye Tela, who was from their homeland, and shared that I had been privileged to go to Nigeria the previous year in order to establish a church planting partnership with an organization within their country. Victoria and Kayode listened intently, as they had never previously known of a church with more than forty nationalities within its membership. The couple and their three children attended the next Sunday service and immediately became involved in the ministries of the church.

This family arrived in 2013 as the fortunate recipients of a visa lottery held in Nigeria. Immediately, they made plans to relocate to the United States for what Victoria described as "greener pastures." Upon arrival, Victoria's family lived with friends they had known from Africa.

Part of Victoria's adjustment to her new living arrangement was the lack of public transportation available in the suburbs. They had been accustomed to city transit giving them access to shopping areas, business buildings, doctors' offices, and other community institutions to meet all of their needs. "How could

such a populated area in the outskirts of Atlanta not have sufficient infrastructure to address these basic human needs?" Victoria
wondered. This inability to navigate their new surroundings left
their family dependent on the benevolent spirit of neighbors and
friends to get groceries, find a way to work, seek medical attention, or tend to any other critical need.

Once established in new jobs, they ventured out to live in
an apartment of their own. All they had brought with them to
America were the things they could fit into a few suitcases; their
apartment was furnished with blankets on the floor and a few
items for the kitchen. Kayode had been an accountant and book-
keeper during their years in Nigeria. Their family had lived an
above-average standard of living back in their country of origin.
These humble beginnings in their new country could have been
disheartening. Victoria, however, describes their gratitude for
God's provisions and how He has met their every need. Like
the Tela family, Victoria and Kayode learned to lean on their
neighbors.

Today, Kayode uses his accounting skills by serving on the
budget committee of the church. Recently, he was ordained as a
deacon in the fellowship, and Victoria is serving in the children's
ministry area. Both have also offered aid in planning and imple-
menting our annual Celebrate Africa Sunday to recognize all of
our African friends and neighbors.

Upon coming to Duluth, Victoria and Kayode were totally
reliant upon the handful of people that they previously knew
from Nigeria as well as the kindness of strangers. Seeing the
emphasis of addressing the needs of newcomers has attracted this
precious family to be completely invested in this multicultural

church. There are numerous African churches available in our area, including ones with Nigerian-born pastors. In fact, one of my neighbors is a Nigerian-born pastor of a Nigerian immigrant church. Victoria says that she is often asked by Nigerian friends why her family chose a multicultural church over a congregation composed of her native people. She says, "My simple answer is that I will not be separated based upon my race, color of my skin, or my language when I arrive in heaven. Why shouldn't I share my experience of worshiping God through Jesus Christ with others now? I enjoy multicultural worship because it reminds me of what heaven will look like when we see God face-to-face in the last days."

I believe that if more church leaders and church members in our nation understood the immigration stories, the immense changes, and the sense of isolation that immigrants experience as they are dispersed into places foreign to them, we would all be moved to visit with them, offer our support, and invite them into our places of worship. Our omniscient Savior Jesus knows every immigrant and refugee backstory, and He has chosen to weave our personal histories together, placing us in the same neighborhoods at this appointed time "so that they might seek God, and perhaps they might reach out and find him, though he is not far from each one of us" (Acts 17:27).

▼ ▼ ▼

CHAPTER FIVE

I Vow Jesus!

Accommodation | Consideration | Acculturation

*For through him we both have access in one spirit
to the Father. So, then, you are no longer foreigners
and strangers, but fellow citizens with the saints, and
members of God's household. (Ephesians 2:18–19)*

*My fellow citizens of the world, ask not what
America can do for you, but what together we can
do for the freedom of man. (John F. Kennedy)*

The word *access* is used only three times in the New Testament.
It is a powerful picture word that describes how a court official would grant someone an audience with the king. Every time
the word is found in Scripture it is in reference to gaining access
to God. I have had the wonderful privilege of being a guest

at numerous naturalization ceremonies where members of my church were being sworn in as United States citizens. Their new status grants them "access" to rights and privileges that are unique to the citizens of this country. When one becomes a believer in the Lord Jesus, new rights are granted, including "access" to the Father and citizenship in heaven.

The measures of a technicolor church are not the numeric data of diversity within the congregation. The success of a multi-cultural church is determined by its ability to grant "access" for all people, all ethnicities, to hear the life-changing message of the gospel. A Lifeway Research project in 2016 indicated that 86 percent of Christians think believers should take care of refugees and foreigners. However, only 19 percent are aware of any ministries provided by their church to address this need. When asked about the discrepancy between the conviction and the reality, 44 percent said the primary reason for inactivity is "fear of global refugees coming to the United States." That adds up to the reality that American churchgoers are twice as likely to fear a foreigner as to care for one.[13]

Step Four: Accommodation

There is a critical distinction between *assimilation* and *accommodation* when it comes to caring for all ethnicities in our congregations. Churches tend to be proponents of assimilation. I have even seen a church staff title: "Minister of Assimilation." This person was responsible for aiding newcomers in learning the culture and values of the church. The concept of assimilation is this: if you are willing to become like us, you can become one of us. Although most churches will not put it quite this bluntly, it is reflected in the songs they sing, the traditions they observe, and the way they receive new members. One well-meaning member once told me, "We really like things the way they are. Try not to change anything!" Churches typically reach people who are most like themselves.

On the other hand, "accommodation" shifts from favoring the dominant culture and honors all cultures and individuals as valuable contributors. *Where are you from? What is important to you? What motivates or discourages you?* With this information, the accommodating church will seek ways to address the needs of the individual. Every culture group has unique qualities that can be accentuated for the betterment of all. At First Baptist Duluth, we celebrate a different culture group each month. Oftentimes, this is a recognition of a cultural holiday or national celebration. In the last chapter, I mentioned that Anna was invited to First Baptist Duluth for an East Asian New Year service, and Victoria and Kayode are instrumental in planning the annual Celebrate Africa Sunday. These celebrations are not only honoring to our members of particular backgrounds but also provide opportunities to reach out to ethnic neighbors within our community and invite them to experience our diverse Christian community and the love of Christ at the center of it.

Dr. Danny McCain, a missionary and professor of world religions in Jos, Nigeria, has relatives in our congregation and visits with us several times a year. Dr. McCain says, "Essentially, this is a missionary enterprise. Many who have come here are leaders in their native countries. Many of them can go back and forth creating bridges to their homeland for evangelism and supporting churches. If I came back to America to pastor a church, I would want it to look like this one. My wife and I have been well-received, and we are not even Baptists; we come from a Methodist/ Wesleyan background. The same people who reach out to people of different ethnicities also will reach out to people of different denominational backgrounds. This is a place where I would feel comfortable bringing an unbeliever from any background. This church has ministered to Muslims, Hindus, Buddhists, and Jews. As a person who has spent more than thirty years overseas trying to reach people of different cultures, I was very pleased when I saw someone doing this kind of ministry in the States."

The ministry of First Baptist Duluth is building bridges to overseas mission fields. Many of the internationals who attend are leaders and they go back and forth between here and their native lands, carrying what they have learned at First Baptist Duluth to their families and friends. The ministry of First Baptist Duluth is a mission collaboration that is touching multiple continents with the good news of Jesus Christ.

David Baba, who was raised as a Muslim in Afghanistan, lost his vision in a work accident and went to India to have a critical surgery to repair his retinal damage. During surgery, David received a different kind of vision: he saw Jesus in a dream. In that dream, Jesus told David to wake up, that He had already healed his eyes. Upon release from the hospital, David sought a pastor or priest who could explain this vision to him. Under the leadership of a Christian minister in India, David prayed to receive Christ. David attended that Indian church for months before eventually returning to his native Afghanistan. He relocated to the United States in 2012 with a refugee resettlement agency.

On the Sunday prior to Christmas each year, I recruit three people who have recently joined our church who speak a language other than or in addition to English. These three and I work together to share a very special global view of Communion. When I asked David if he would lead us by reading his portion in Farsi, he was both delighted and overwhelmed by the opportunity. On the morning of the service, David appeared exceptionally nervous. I found him off in a corner of the sanctuary practicing his lines as if he were memorizing them. I tried to explain to David that memorizing his lines was not required. It was perfectly acceptable for him to read his part. There is only one other Farsi speaker in the church, and I was sure she would be fine with his rendering. David nodded in agreement, but continued to rehearse his lines for the Communion.

David's English is rudimentary at best. However, after the service he came to explain to me his dilemma. We were struggling to communicate when one of our ministry interns, Charlotte Kumar, intervened. Fluent in several Indian dialects, Charlotte attempted to interpret for David. I was astounded at Charlotte's abilities and asked if she was fluent in David's native language, Farsi. She said, "No, we are speaking in Hindi. He learned the language during his time in India." She explained to me that though David speaks his language fluently, his literacy was limited due to Al-Qaeda preventing many students from attending school in his region. The group controls who can receive an education so that they can govern the flow of information to the people. Charlotte and David continued on in conversation. I waited anxiously to get the interpretation. I soon came to understand that David was sharing his conversion story and his connection to India. Suddenly, Charlotte squealed with delight. David had told her the name of the pastor who had led him to Christ. Charlotte recognized the name immediately as a longtime friend of their family. David would later share his conversion testimony in a church service with Charlotte as interpreter. You might be in a multicultural church if a Farsi-speaking former Muslim from Afghanistan is speaking in Hindi utilizing the interpretation skills of a ministry intern from India!

KJ Lee, our current chairman of deacons, soon adopted David as a discipleship partner. The two of them have been meeting every Friday night for a couple of years. KJ, a native of Korea, is attempting to learn Farsi as David continues his pilgrimage to English proficiency. This past year David was wed as the result of an arranged marriage by his family back in Afghanistan. KJ is teaching David the Scriptures, but he is also mentoring David as a new husband and in every aspect of life. Where would David receive this kind of attention had it not been for the accommodating spirit of the First Baptist Duluth?

Step Five: Consideration

Due to the receptive, welcoming nature of our church, it is not unusual on any given Sunday for our church to have guests who are Muslim, Hindu, Buddhist, or even atheist. People are searching for truth! And they are looking for a community of faith that is open to discussing their questions.

Mae is from China. She and her husband have lived in several metro cities in America, including San Diego and Dallas. When the family learned of their relocation to Atlanta, Mae chose to live in our suburban area because of the large Chinese population that enables them to find Chinese grocery stores and other pleasant reminders of home.

Mae first came to First Baptist Duluth to enroll her twin daughters in our weekday preschool. Mae echoes the philosophy of many in China when she says, "I believe in science and do not have a religion," but she was not opposed to her girls being educated in a "diverse environment." One day when she picked up her children from school, she noticed a flyer in her children's take-home papers. The preschool families were invited to participate in the church's celebration of Tres Reyes Magos (Three Kings Day), a Latino celebration after Christmas that commemorates the coming of the wise men to worship the Christ child. Mae's daughters pleaded with her to allow them to attend this special day. Mae called a couple of Chinese friends, and they decided to attend the service together.

Mae said, "Back in China I never visited a church; there were so few." She had once toured a church building in the United States, but this would be her first experience in a Christian worship service. As she entered the building, she was amazed at the incredible diversity of the church family. Her eyes were drawn to the forty-seven flags perched around the perimeter of the auditorium representing the makeup of the First Baptist Duluth congregation. She commented to her friends that the church provides free childcare on Sundays so that adults can be involved in Bible study. And on her first Sunday, she participated in a meal after the service, joining the Latino portion of the congregation in their cultural way of celebrating Christmas.

Soon after that first church experience, Mae became involved in a Sunday morning Bible study group specifically designed for students with rudimentary English skills. Two of our volunteers, Barbara Curnutt and Grace Woodard, took the initiative to start a weekday group that would answer questions that many students from non-Christian backgrounds were asking. Mae has become a regular at this discipleship offering. Mae said, "I knew that God and the Bible were key to the American culture, but before I could follow God, I needed to learn about Him."

Mae has become involved in English classes and cooking classes at church, as well as Bible studies on Sunday and Tuesday. She says, "Before I attended First Baptist Duluth, I had no local friends. I only got out of the house to go shopping. Life was boring! But now I have a lot of friends and things to do. Life is good!" When Mae recently made a trip back to China to visit family, her discipleship group came to her home to bid her farewell and pray for her safety in travels. "Before coming to the church, I lived in a Chinese bubble," says Mae. She now is seeking truth alongside a group of diverse friends who genuinely care for her and are accepting of where she is on her faith journey.

The official religious category for Mae is called "none." When asked on a survey question to state their religious preference, these people do not check a box that says "agnostic" or "atheist"; they simply choose "none of the above." This relatively new category of religious indifference is sweeping America. The "nones" are the fastest-growing religious preference in the United States. Mae, who was once a "none," now says, "I believe there is a God and I need to respect Him. I am still learning!" I once heard a pastor refer to evangelistic prospects as "pre-Christian." We have experienced a great number of people who are not ready to make a conversion decision but are incredibly open to the gospel and grateful for our willingness to teach them.

One hot summer day a woman wearing a head covering appeared at our church office doors in the middle of a weekday. Becky Sproles, our volunteer receptionist, greeted our guest and quickly discerned that she struggled with English. The woman had walked a considerable distance in the Georgia sun to enroll in the church's English program at the recommendation of a friend. Halimeh and her husband, Ali, emigrated from Iran in 2012. They have two adult children and now that they are on their own, Halimeh felt it was time to apply herself to working diligently on her English proficiency. Becky had the unenviable task of informing our visitor that our English classes took a summer break and would not start up again for over a month. Halimeh was disappointed to learn the news, but thanked Becky for the information and began to walk home. When Becky learned that Halimeh would be walking back in the hot sun, she invited her to stay in the air-conditioned building until noon, when Becky could finish her shift and give Halimeh a ride home. Becky arranged a comfortable space next to her at the receptionist desk and told Halimeh they could practice English during her wait. Becky had some previous exposure to Muslim people. Years earlier, her family lived in Saudi Arabia for her husband, Robert's, job. This delighted Halimeh, that her impromptu tutor had at least some knowledge of her culture group.

When Becky dropped Halimeh off at her home, Halimeh asked if she could return the next day to sit and practice her English. Becky explained that her volunteer position was only on Wednesday mornings and that it would be next week before she would again be at the front desk. Halimeh smiled and said, "I will see you next Wednesday."

On the following Wednesday when I arrived at the office, I greeted Becky at the reception desk and was somewhat surprised to see a small-statured lady with a head covering sitting next to her. Becky quickly offered introductions: "Pastor, this is Halimeh. We are working on her English." I greeted Halimeh and then walked into the office suite and tried to find someone who could give me the backstory of what I had just witnessed. These personal English tutoring sessions persisted weekly for the remainder of the summer. It was such a blessing to greet Halimeh every week and watch her grow in confidence with her language skills as well as becoming comfortable in her new setting.

As the two got to know each other, Becky asked Halimeh if she had ever read the Bible. She responded that she had never owned a Bible of her own. Becky checked with our Language Resource Center which is stocked with Bibles in twenty-five different languages. Becky found a copy in Farsi and provided Halimeh her own personal copy of the Scriptures in her language. Becky was making great progress with Halimeh's English skills as well as answering key questions that Halimeh had about our faith. One morning Halimeh asked Becky if we taught the Bible at our church. Amused at the question, Becky responded that yes, we teach the Bible every Sunday. Halimeh pressed further, asking if Becky herself was involved with teaching the Bible at the church. Becky answered that she was a teacher in the children's department, teaching young people the Bible stories, often for the very first time. Halimeh looked at her tutor and innocently declared, "I have never heard the Bible stories." After that, Becky came to me and asked permission to have Halimeh sit in our fifth-grade Sunday school class as an observer. She prepared her class that an adult who was learning English wanted to join their group and that she had a desire to learn from the Bible. The class was elated to welcome their new member. Halimeh sat weekly, absorbing spiritual knowledge like a sponge.

After several weeks of Sunday school class, Becky asked Halimeh if she would like to attend a worship service. Unsure, Halimeh asked what transpired during a typical worship service. Becky put her mind at ease and explained that, like Sunday school, there would be a Bible lesson and that the congregation of people from many different backgrounds would sing and pray together. Halimeh agreed to attend the next week *if* she could sit with Becky. Halimeh sat alongside Becky, writing notes about things she would discuss with her teacher after the service. At the conclusion of every service, my wife, Glenda, and I host a "meet the pastor" time in our church's International Grounds Café. There, Glenda and Halimeh formed a special bond. Soon, they were spending time together doing special things like cooking together in preparation for Easter. This gave Glenda an opportunity to reinforce Becky's teachings and communicate to Halimeh the importance of the Easter message.

It was incredible to watch Halimeh hunger for more and more knowledge about Jesus. Every Sunday she attended she would stop by the café to greet Glenda and me. On one occasion, she was trying to get my attention. However, due to her limited English proficiency, I could not understand what she was trying to say to me. With a sense of urgency, she pulled out her smartphone and typed the Farsi script into a Google Translate app. She then turned the phone to face me. It read: "I vow Jesus." This Iranian Muslim woman had been trying to declare to me that she now believes in Jesus Christ. Halimeh still believes in all her Muslim teachings. She is trying to reconcile her budding Christian faith with a lifetime of traditions, but she is confessing that Jesus is real and that she has encountered Him.

In November of 2019, my wife, Glenda, was scheduled to have major back surgery. The entire church had been asked to pray for this event. When we arrived at the hospital that morning, they took Glenda to a surgery prep area and asked me to stay in the family waiting room. Nurses assured me that I would be able to come and see her one more time before the procedure began. As I settled in the waiting room, I noticed someone entering immediately behind me. When I turned, I saw Halimeh entering. I learned that her husband, Ali, was having surgery on the same day. Halimeh and I prayed together, and then we sat together awaiting news about our spouses. In a short while, a nurse came to retrieve me to come to the pre-op area to see Glenda. Halimeh asked if she could join me and come and pray for her friend. When we turned the corner to enter the room, Glenda saw that I had a guest with me. She smiled from ear to ear as Halimeh came and knelt beside her bed and began to kiss her hand. She asked, "Could I pray for you, Ms. Glenda?" And without hesitation, she spontaneously began to pray. Halimeh begged the God of healing to come and touch her friend "in Jesus' name." I could barely fight back the tears of this beautiful picture of God's redemptive power.

As Glenda headed into the surgical suite, Halimeh and I sat to visit for the remainder of the morning in the waiting room. I asked Halimeh if Ali would be open to receiving a visit from me after surgery. She was delighted that I would drop by. The next morning, I stopped by Ali's room. Their adult son and daughter were also present. After a short visit, I asked if I could pray for Ali. He agreed for me to do so. At the conclusion of my prayer, he asked me how long my wife and I have been married. I proudly reported that we would soon celebrate our fortieth year of marriage. Ali turned to his children and admonished them: "Marry a Christian. They know how to keep their promises." Did I just hear a Muslim man instruct his children to consider marrying outside their tradition?

I am reminded of the words of the prophet Joel:

> Multitudes, multitudes
> in the valley of decision!
> For the day of the LORD is near
> in the valley of decision. (Joel 3:14)

The ministry of First Baptist Duluth has abundant opportunities to walk people through the "valley of decision." We are learning the mindset shifts necessary for people to embrace Christ and become a part of His family. I am blessed to be the messenger and be engaged in the process.

Step Six: Acculturation

Edith's parents divorced when she was eight years old. Shortly thereafter, her mother left Edith and her siblings with relatives in Mexico and went to the United States, promising to retrieve her family as soon as it was feasible. As a child, Edith's Catholic

Church affiliation was more identified with her culture than her faith. In the summer of her seventh-grade year, she was invited to a Seventh Day Adventist Camp, where she responded to the gospel and came to know Jesus as her Savior. Edith was fourteen when she first came to the United States and was reunited with her mother. She deeply desired a stable family structure, a cultural identity, and a sense of belonging.

Edith's husband, Luis, had come to America to work and send aid to his struggling family back in Mexico. Edith and Luis met in 2008 and moved to Duluth in 2009 to be near relatives and seek stable employment. Luis had never attended church in Mexico. Edith, however, began to search for a faith family that would meet her needs and provide a spiritual foundation for her newborn daughter, Rihanna. Their first church family was a Spanish-speaking congregation. Edith felt that, due to Luis's limited English skills, there would be a higher likelihood that he would attend this church than others in the area. But due to a lack of young families with children, Edith did not feel very connected to the church. As Rihanna grew to elementary school age, Edith knew that she needed to find a church they could call home and aid in her child's spiritual development. Edith's mother had been visiting a church that she thought would be a good fit for her daughter and granddaughter. That was our church, and in 2013, Edith brought Rihanna to visit.

At first, Edith was apprehensive about how her family would fit in at an English-speaking church. She recalls how she was so intimidated on a daily basis as a Spanish speaker trying to fit in an English world that she did not at first realize that the church was multicultural and actually had a variety of different language groups within it. Edith's daughter, Rihanna, fell in love with her Sunday school class filled with children from all over the world. She told her mother about how they sing, play, and study together as one group. Rihanna was rapidly becoming attached to the First Baptist Duluth family. She began to plead with her father, Luis, to join the family in worship service, telling him that the services are interpreted into Spanish and that there would be people from many nations present. Luis began to attend and soon joined a First Class where congregants learn how to become a member of the church. Neither Edith nor Luis had ever been baptized by immersion, a requirement for church membership after one testifies of a personal relationship with Christ. Through an interpreter I was able to discern that Luis had invited Jesus into his life and that he and Edith now desired to follow through with baptism. Edith asked if our children's director would talk with Rihanna and see if she was ready to join her parents in this faith journey. It was my wonderful privilege to baptize this entire family on a celebratory Sunday morning.

After baptism, Edith immersed herself in the life of the church. She and Luis took a CROSS Class, and after that, they joined a Connection Group, a biweekly supper group that welcomes newcomers into the church and helps them find ways to get connected. This couple, once timid about stepping out of their language-centric environment, were now finding themselves totally transformed into ambassadors for cross-cultural ministry. Edith says, "I am enjoying my new family in Christ, where I feel loved and welcome."

What prepared Jeffrey Go's wife, Anna, for her involvement in this church was a deep longing as a result of unmet needs.

As a child of Korean immigrants living in Wisconsin, Anna grew up going to a Korean Presbyterian church where almost everyone looked like her, but she often felt like the odd one out. She had grown to expect that she would never truly fit in or feel fully loved at any church. As a young couple, she and Jeffrey had attended megachurches where the services were outstanding, but no one knew them personally. When they found the vibrant multicultural congregation at First Baptist Duluth, Anna started feeling more at home than at any other time or place in her life. She found people living out the all-too-rare reality of "they will know we are Christians by our love." Those attitudes are contagious. "Our love for Jesus makes us love who He loves," Anna said. "I love love! There are so many lonely people. I know what that feels like, and now I know what it feels like to receive attention and love, so I want to pass it along to someone else." The way people have loved Anna into the church makes her want to do the same for others. Anna has begun volunteering with our English classes, serving people like Halimeh, who does not yet claim Christ as Savior, but is growing in her knowledge and love of Jesus.

First Baptist Duluth embraces internationals with their unique cultural nuances and celebrates the value that each of us brings to the faith community. We are not seeking to assimilate people into a prescribed mold, but rather accommodating our diverse friends to express themselves in their chosen ways. As a result of our openness to diversity, God has given us the glorious opportunity to impact people who come from a variety of different religious backgrounds, including those who choose "none" as their religious preference. This impact has grown to fruition in seeing people who were once intimidated by cultural differences now become participants and proponents. This is the type of faith family that people from every culture are seeking!

CHAPTER SIX

▼ ▼ ▼

Is This a Cult?

Redemption | Dedication | Commission

*"May they all be one, as you, Father, are in me and
I am in you. May they also be in us, so that the
world may believe you sent me." (John 17:21)*

*Every heart with Christ is a missionary, every heart
without Christ is a mission field. (Nicolaus Zinzendorf)*

W e are living in possibly the most divisive time period in our
history. The nation is completely gridlocked by partisan
politics. Not since the Civil War have political ideologies caused
such deep rifts. This emotionally charged division has formed
an accepted and anticipated reality that we will always have "us"
versus "them." This has caused people to be divided over even the
most minimal differences in personal preference.

This acquiescence to live in a divided society has affected the evangelical church for a long time. In 1963, Rev. Martin Luther King Jr. declared Sunday mornings at 11:00 a.m. as the "most segregated hour in America." More than fifty years later, eight out of every ten churches in our nation are composed primarily of one single ethnic group. In a 2015 Lifeway study on segregation of churches, 67 percent of those surveyed felt their church was "doing enough" to be ethnically diverse. Unfortunately, the modern-day church is not seeing the tremendous door of opportunity that is opening to gospel proliferation. The greatest evangelistic tool we possess in a globalizing society is an ethnically diverse people coming together as one. The world is willing to give an audience when unity meets diversity.

Step Seven: Redemption

Like many immigrants, Li says that her family came to the United States to give their children a better life. In 2017, Li and her husband opened a map of the United States and began to contemplate where this adventure would take them. She says they chose Duluth because of the educational opportunities, strong economy, and mild climate. Their transition would be made easier by the fact that our community is home to a large Chinese/Asian population that provides many comforts familiar to them.

Upon moving from China, Li's first impression was how incredibly green her new surroundings had become. "I felt like I was now living in a forest," she laughs. Although she enjoyed her new setting, Li and her family remained mostly secluded due to their limited English skills. Simple tasks like getting gas or going to the bank were complicated ordeals for her and her family. She sought the aid of other Chinese homemakers in the area to acclimate herself and found some camaraderie and friendship.

One of those newfound friends encouraged Li to enroll her son and daughter in the weekday preschool at First Baptist Duluth. Li discovered that the student body at the school was as diverse as the community where she now resided. She enthusiastically sent her children to their new school knowing they would have chapel, learn Bible stories, and sing scriptural songs daily. On one occasion, her daughter asked for forgiveness for a misdeed she'd committed at home. Li responded that she had already forgiven her. Her daughter responded, "Oh, like Peter did!" Li thought to herself: *Who is Peter and what does he have to do with my forgiveness of my daughter?* Her daughter proceeded to tell the Bible story from her chapel lesson, sharing the conversation from Matthew 18:21–22: "Then Peter approached him and asked, 'Lord, how many times must I forgive my brother or sister who sins against me? As many as seven times?' 'I tell you, not as many as seven,' Jesus replied, 'but seventy times seven.'" Later in the same school year, her daughter asked about the meaning of the holiday, "Good Friday." Li told her it must be "good" because you don't have to go to school. Li's inability to answer her daughter's questions started a journey of discovery for her.

Friends invited Li to attend our church alongside them. However, Li felt self-conscious and unsure about how to participate in a church service. She reasoned: "I am not a Christian, I have never read the Bible, and I am limited in my ability to communicate." Li was fearful of unknown rules and restrictions and wondered if she might inadvertently cross a line. However, after much coaxing, she attended a service. Li admits that, at first, she thought Christianity, the Bible, and church were things beyond her reach. She had yet to realize that those "who were far away have been brought near by the blood of Jesus Christ" (Eph. 2:13).

Li joined a Sunday morning Bible study group designed for people with limited English proficiency. Li says it was in that class where she learned to pray and believe in God. Back in China, Li and her husband did not practice any religion. Li was absorbing spiritual truth and wanted more. She instructed her children that they needed to faithfully attend church and learn as much as possible. Attempting to become more proficient in English, Li passed up the opportunity to use a device to hear the sermons in her native Mandarin. However, she did take advantage of the Mandarin sermon note sheets provided and followed along as well as she could. Li's husband does not attend church with the family, but he does support their participation and says he has noticed a change in how grateful the children seem to be.

Dr. Jeremy Sin, a missionary with the North American Mission Board, is one of the volunteer workers in the remedial English Bible class. Noticing the exceptional hunger and growth in Li, he asked if he could disciple her and a few other class members in what it means to become a Christian. Li was thrilled to enter this process, and within the week, Dr. Sin led Li to a faith relationship with Jesus. In December of 2019, I had the immense privilege of baptizing Li as a new believer in Jesus Christ. Li describes the joy of her newfound faith: "I have a sense of belonging. We have no family in the United States, but now First Baptist Duluth has become our family."

We have tried to be faithful to Li as a new family member. In 2020, the world suffered the devastations of COVID-19. Li's husband was traveling on business in China when the airlines shut down all transcontinental flights. Li and her husband were separated for several grueling months while awaiting travel options. During this frightening time, Li found that her church family would pray for her, encourage her, care for her and her children, and give her an inexplicable sense of peace. Li says that through this crisis she has learned the meaning of an American colloquialism: "I have your back." Li has experienced that one can trust in God and have strength and peace regardless of the circumstances . . . and that God's people have her back!

Step Eight: Dedication

Easter Sunday 2018 was a glorious day of celebration at First Baptist Duluth. The sanctuary was filled with people who had come to experience the power of the resurrected Christ. That morning, we also dedicated the opening of our One Voice Language Resource Center, a ministry that offers interpretation, Bible distribution, and English lessons for all of the language groups that make up our congregation and community. In my previous book, *Technicolor*, I shared the story of Robert and Pamela Buziba, a Ugandan couple I was privileged to lead to a salvation experience. The Buzibas gifted me a beautiful piece of colorful cloth called a "kanga." Robert explained to me that the kanga is an African garment that symbolizes hospitality. It is worn around the house much like an apron. Every "kanga" has a Swahili proverb written upon it. This particular cloth was inscribed with *Upendo wa mungu umetuweka pamoja*, meaning, "The love of God has brought us together."

I asked the Buzibas if I could frame the kanga and place it on display in the Language Resource Center. After receiving permission, I had the kanga professionally framed with a matting around its border. On Easter morning during the worship service, I shared the story of the Buzibas' conversion and their meaningful gift. While the congregation was singing, I invited every person who spoke a language other than English to come forward and autograph the matting around the kanga in their native tongue. It was incredible to witness more than a hundred people who stood in line awaiting the opportunity to make this declaration of the unity that God brings within the body of Christ.

As I greeted parishioners and guests after the service, I met a delightful couple who were attending for the very first time. Both Ray and Judy are 1.5-generation immigrants from China. First-generation immigrants were born in a foreign country. Second-generation immigrants were born in the United States and their parents were born in a foreign country. However, 1.5-generations were brought to the United States as children and identify more with American culture than their parents, often becoming immersed in English and dropping the ability to speak their native language. Ray had moved to the United States at the age of seven, and Judy had come at the age of twelve. Both were educated in the United States, and they met as college coeds at Georgia Tech in Atlanta, where they both were studying to become engineers.

Ray's parents divorced when he was a child. His mother remarried when he was fourteen, and his new stepdad moved the family from San Francisco, California, to Greenville, South Carolina, for his business. There was not a great deal of diversity in the Greenville school system. Ray was one of only four Asians in his entire high school. However, Ray was befriended by a young man who would lead him to Christ during his senior year. When I heard Ray share his testimony, he thanked God for moving him to the South. There may not have been an abundance of diversity, but there was a clear opportunity to hear about Jesus.

Upon high school graduation, Ray moved to the Georgia Tech campus. There, he met, dated, and fell in love with Judy. Ray and Judy both hung around several friends who followed Jesus, but Judy credits Ray with leading her into a faith relationship. Upon graduation, Ray and Judy married and started an engineering business together and eventually watched their family grow with the addition of two sons to their home. They desired to lead their children by example, faithfully attending a church. As their boys grew, Ray and Judy became actively engaged as volunteers in the youth ministry of a Chinese church in our area. This culture-centric church was bilingual with services offered in Mandarin and English. Recalling his own high school experience, Ray wanted his sons to be well-grounded in their faith. As he observed the diversification of the community and the schools that his sons attended, Ray became uneasy with a culture-centric church setting. In his personal research, he Googled the phrase "multicultural church" and discovered a book titled *Technicolor: Inspiring Your Church to Embrace Multicultural Ministry*. He ordered a copy and, upon its arrival, began reading with interest the story of our church's transition from monocultural congregation to multicultural community of faith.

Ray shared with Judy the stories he was gleaning from his reading about this church that has more than forty nationalities within its membership. Judy recalled that during her time spent in California, some churches were organically diverse based upon the diverse population of their area. However, she could not recall any that had the kind of diversity that brought African, Asian, Latino, European, and local cultures together under one roof to worship. She asked Ray, "Where is this church?" He told her the church was in Duluth, less than fifteen minutes from their home. So, Judy surmised that there could only be one explanation for this phenomenon: "So, is it a cult?" Ray responded that he did not think there was anything doctrinally off-base from his reading, but would like to see this church in person. The couple began to make plans to attend the Easter worship service.

When the Lees introduced themselves to my wife and me, Ray shared that he had just completed my book and wanted to see the congregation firsthand. They witnessed the dedication of the Language Resource Center and saw the outpouring of diverse people who are regularly gathering at First Baptist Duluth. I thanked Ray for reading *Technicolor* and offered an invitation for them to join us at our home the following Tuesday evening for our CROSS Class. I told my inquisitive visitors that this would provide them a "behind the curtain look" into the makeup of the congregation. Here, they would meet newcomers from around the globe who are currently attending First Baptist Duluth. The two looked at each other and said that they would make a concerted effort to attend.

Tuesday was the first meeting of the six-week gathering for CROSS Class. As people began to arrive, everyone was in the same awkward position of knowing very few people in the room. I was pleased to see the Lees walking up my sidewalk, accepting the invitation to check out the class. The first gathering is a "get to know you" session, providing ample time for every family to tell their story. The Lees listened as people shared their faith journeys as well as the accounts of coming to America and how they wound up attending our church. One of the highlights of CROSS Class is asking participants to share a snack or dessert from their country at the end of each class as an opportunity for fellowship and cultural exchange. When I asked on week one if anyone would bravely step up and volunteer to bring the dessert for week two, the Lees raised their hands. I knew then that God was likely calling Ray and Judy to be a part of our faith family.

Over the next six weeks, Ray and Judy asked questions about the vision and strategy of the church. They found themselves engaged with long-tenured members talking about best practices for reaching people and befriended by immigrant families who wanted to know them on a deeper level. I wondered if, at the conclusion of the class, the Lees would return to their culture-centric church setting with the hope that they could potentially be a catalyst for change there. On the final week of class, we plan a dinner with everyone bringing a food from their native country. This international buffet has become well-known among all who have ever experienced a CROSS Class. At the conclusion of the meal, we have a debriefing time for volunteers to share what God has taught them during the class. Ray and Judy said that the class had fulfilled a spiritual longing in their hearts and that they planned to become a part of the ministry efforts of First Baptist Duluth.

If one wants to eavesdrop on Jesus' prayer life, John 17 is
the place where you'll hear the Savior pour out His heart to the
Father. And what does Jesus pray for? Three times in this passage
Jesus asks the Father that His followers would be one, united in
their passion and purpose:

> "I am in them and you are in me, so that they may be
> made completely one, that the world may know that you
> have sent me and have loved them as you have loved me."
> (v. 23)

This sentence structure in the Greek language is referred to
as a *hina* clause. It is the Greek equivalent to an if/then equation.
If believers in the Lord Jesus Christ live and act in unity, *then* the
world will understand and desire the love of Christ.

In a country that is extremely divided, the testimony of one-
ness is a powerful evangelism tool, especially in a community as
diverse as Duluth. Ray and Judy not only became members of
the church, they became active servants within the church. This
couple has loved taking the gospel outside the walls and into
the community. Ray laments that many culture-centric churches
become myopic in their approach, wanting to "hold on" to the
next generation. However, at First Baptist Duluth, he saw a
church that was intentionally going into the community to reach
the next generation of every culture group! God had placed a
multicultural vision upon Ray and Judy's hearts and now had
given them the means by which to fulfill it. Every person has to
make the decision to step outside the comfort of their culture-
centric world, including English-speaking Anglos. As Ray told

me, "God is bigger than any one culture group. We need to remember, Christ died for all!"

Step Nine: Commission

Jeonghyun (Joseph) Kim and his wife, Youngmi, were married in their native Korea. Joseph had recently finished medical school and was making plans to do international humanitarian work among the impoverished in Nepal. Youngmi's family was Buddhist. They, however, allowed her to attend a Christian high school where she became a believer. She soon began being discipled in a Methodist church. Joseph recalls that his mother was Baptist, but Joseph wanted very little to do with church until he was in college, where he became a Christian. As a new believer, Joseph also began attending a Methodist church. The young couple had both begun their faith with a Methodist background. And yet, upon marriage they began attending a Presbyterian church. During their two and a half years of service in South Asia, Dr. Kim, a physician, was sensing a calling to prepare for a lifetime of international mission service. Joseph and Youngmi would spend long hours praying and planning what their next move would be in pursuit of this God-sized vision that had been placed in their hearts. They concluded that their preparation should include mastering English and engaging in some theological education.

From friends who were already living in our area, Joseph learned of the large Korean population in the suburbs. The young couple began to make plans to locate in the Duluth area. The first experiences in their new adopted home were not all positive ones.

While trying to obtain a driver's license at the DMV, the Kims recall being treated rudely because they did not speak English well. The simple task of having utilities turned on at their apartment became a monumental task because there were few people willing to offer assistance to a foreigner. However, the one place where they were immediately welcomed and felt at home was First Baptist Duluth.

The couple's family had grown with the birth of a son and a daughter. They had attended two different Korean churches during their early years. But Joseph felt that they should step outside of a Korean culture-centric church and possibly find an American church that would expand their horizon. One day they visited a Korean home to complete a transaction for an online purchase they had made. While exchanging pleasantries with the seller of the item, Joseph and Youngmi shared their challenges of living in the new area and their desire for "something different" in a church home. The person listened intently and then offered a recommendation. Although she had never personally been to the church, she had heard of an American church that has a Korean minister on staff, offers interpretation of the worship services, teaches English classes, and has an outstanding weekday preschool program.

The next week, Joseph and Youngmi attended our service. "It didn't take long for us to fall in love with the ministry of the church. On our third week in attendance, we decided that we should become members." In November of 2016, they were baptized. I performed the ordinance with Pastor Tom Rhe, our ministry intern, standing beside me and interpreting. "We had never seen such a diverse gathering of believers. We felt as if we were experiencing heaven on earth," Joseph says. "The thing that unites the church is worship of God and a firm vision."

Upon joining the church, the Kims became involved in every aspect of the ministry. They immediately joined the young adult Bible study class. This dynamic group is led by one of our deacons, Gary Lancaster. This group would become their greatest friends and closest confidants. In their new community of faith, the Kims had now found the missing help they had longed for. The couple fell in love with Gary's teaching and even commented fondly that as they spent time with him, they were learning how to speak with a "Southern accent."

Joseph and Youngmi heard about a six-week class being taught at the pastor's home that would encourage cross-cultural exchange. So, the Kims signed up for the next semester of CROSS Class. After each class session, there is a snack time where one-on-one conversations tend to take place on a much deeper and more profound level. During one such time, Joseph asked me why my wife and I would open our home to all the diverse members of the congregation. He explained that in his tradition, pastors were held in high esteem and not many church members would have access to them. As a matter of fact, this was the first time in his life that he had ever been in the home of a minister. I tried to explain to Joseph the mutual benefit gained by hosting these classes. When we first began the CROSS Class, all the internationals of the church fit inside my living room. This was my time to learn about their culture and, in the process, they were learning about each other. Now, we host the class three times a year with new people coming from around the world. Joseph expressed extreme gratitude at being included in this remarkable gathering.

It was during CROSS Class that the Kims would become best friends with the Buzibas from Uganda. They have three children similar in age to the Kims' two children, and they both lived in the same apartment complex. After the CROSS Class concluded, the Kims and the Buzibas continued sharing a meal together almost every week, introducing the Buzibas to Korean cuisine and the Buzibas likewise teaching the Kims about African delicacies. The two families even vacationed together on a beach trip to Florida. The Buzibas and the Kims have truly become family!

Joseph attempted multiple times to become licensed in the United States to practice medicine. However, he consistently stumbled on the English proficiency portion of the exam. This created a challenge in finding ways to support his family as they continued to pursue the vision of preparing for missionary service. Joseph was delighted to learn that New Orleans Baptist Theological Seminary offers degrees with classes provided in Korean. First Baptist Duluth was the host of the Korean Training Institute of the seminary. Every Monday our church welcomes approximately one hundred theological students as the primary campus for Korean language students. Joseph was able to enroll and attend theological classes, as he had originally planned, and they happened to be hosted within his own church facility!

Over the next four years the Kims became invested in multiple areas of ministry. Youngmi became involved in the food pantry ministry. Every week she worked alongside an amazing group of volunteers who listened to her story and prayed regularly for her family. One senior adult deacon, Ross Gallman, became the family's minister of encouragement. Ross would send Joseph and Youngmi cards and letters reminding them

to remain faithful to their calling. The Kims recall anonymous cash gifts that often came at just the right time to meet a need in their family budget.

In the meantime, Joseph was offering his services to the remedial English Bible study. He was able to connect with Korean speakers and help them to navigate their way into active church life. He also became a member of the church's missions committee. First Baptist Duluth supports several church planters in inner-city Atlanta, as well as church planting programs in four other countries: Nigeria, China, Mexico, and India. The mission committee plans trips to support and encourage these works. In February of 2019, the committee was planning to conduct a health clinic with our partners in India. During this trip we would establish a relationship with a new partner in the strategic city of Varanasi, considered one of the holiest places for people of the Hindu religion. Joseph recalled his days doing humanitarian work in Nepal and immediately volunteered to be a part of the team.

Dr. Kim was not licensed to practice medicine in India. However, he worked alongside an Indian physician from a Hindu background to minister to hundreds of needy people in the slums. The team experienced the darkness of Varanasi, a city on the banks of the Ganges River. Many nationals take a pilgrimage to the city near the end of their life so that after death they may have their body burned and buried in the holy river. Streets are filled with people lacking hope and desiring death. This trip escalated Joseph's heart for missionary work. He returned grateful for the opportunity and desiring next steps to meet his personal missionary calling. In the fall of 2019, Joseph was elected a deacon of

First Baptist Duluth, recognizing his incredible servant leadership within the body.

Because of Joseph's inability to become a licensed physician in the States, he was not capable of reducing his student debt and preparing his family for international service. After much prayer, the Kims made the difficult decision to return to Korea for a time, allowing Joseph to practice medicine and prepare his family financially for their future missionary service. This was a painful process for the Kims as well as for our church family. Rather than feeling like they were headed home, the Kims felt like they were leaving home. We miss them. The four years spent with us in Duluth had created a "home church" for the Kims and turned us into a "sending church" that they will remain connected to for the rest of their lives.

Joseph likens First Baptist Duluth to the church at Antioch in the book of Acts. The Antioch church was noted for its diversity. It was also known to be the sending church that created the missionary team of Paul and Barnabas. Joseph and Youngmi had witnessed the heart of First Baptist Duluth's ministry to the "foreigner and the immigrant." Upon arrival back in Korea, Joseph viewed his homeland through new eyes. Joseph says, "We are searching for the marginalized among us. We are hoping that God will use us to meet the needs of others." I am reminded of the apostle Paul's advice to his young protégé, Timothy:

What you have heard from me in the presence of many witnesses, commit to faithful men who will be able to teach others also. (2 Tim. 2:2)

Joseph summarizes his time in Duluth: "For those who are going to visit First Baptist Duluth, they will see heaven in this church: every nation, tribe, people, and language group praising and serving one true God. My family hopes to serve as missionaries and lead people of various cultures to experience that same unifying relationship with God." The Kims' move to Korea was an emotional time for our church, but we have not lost a family. Instead, we have multiplied our ministry into a new area and another continent. The ultimate goal of the multicultural church is not to be a collection of ethnicities but rather to become an incubator for missionaries in our local community and around the world.

SECTION THREE

Leaders

Vision | Devotion | Action

Inclusion | Communication | Determination

Reconciliation | Collaboration | Education

▼ ▼ ▼

CHAPTER SEVEN

The Die Is Cast

Vision | Devotion | Action

Everyone should look not to his own interests, but
rather to the interests of others. (Philippians 2:4)

Our main business is not to see what lies
dimly at a distance, but to do what lies
clearly at hand. (Thomas Carlyle)

Any hiker who has ever ventured off the main path will testify of scrapes, scratches, and sometimes worse from choosing to enter uncharted territory. Georgia Baptist Executive Thomas Hammond says, "Pioneers have scars. When you are the first, you are logging all these different experiences. The early explorer gets the bug bites and snakebites so that later travelers can avoid them. . . . The one who ventures first must be willing to experience the hurts and pains of the unknown." This has been the nature of the ministry at First Baptist Duluth. Preparing a church for multicultural ministry is not an easy task. Hammond commends the church's stalwart practices and patient perseverance, saying, "Relationships take time. The church is creating an entirely new culture that welcomes the nations among them."

Navigating this changing environment is affecting the churches of our state. Hammond recently gave the following illustration: "Cassette tapes were once selling like crazy. Then came the introduction of CDs, but nobody had CD players yet. Then along came MP3s and made both cassettes and CDs obsolete. In the midst of the coronavirus pandemic, the companies that have survived are the ones that were most prepared for the future. The ones that have crashed and burned are the ones that wanted to return to the way things used to be. A great number of churches today are stuck in the past and unwilling to change. Churches today are still trying to use 'boom box' methods to reach an MP3 world."

I have spent the past ten years growing our church's vision by surrounding myself with staff who have discerned the same call from God, seeking the wisdom of pioneers in the multicultural movement, and partnering with community leaders and religious workers who can give valuable insight and opportunities for growth. The last section of this book will tell their stories. Each of them is unique in their personal calling to multicultural work, but they follow a similar path to ultimately doing technicolor ministry.

Step One: Vision

Todd Jones grew up in Metro Atlanta, where there was a church at almost every major intersection, some of them a hundred years old or more. Soaring steeples have long been the landmarks of this community. As many local churches have been busy figuring out how to survive and serve their aging congregations, the landscape has been changing. When Atlanta opened itself to the world with the 1996 Olympic Games, international interests in the area grew exponentially in the late '90s and early 2000s. Old strip malls came to life with new ethnic restaurants and businesses. This has created a cultural tsunami as Gwinnett County was 96 percent White in 1980 and is 39 percent White today.[14] It wasn't only the business scene that was changing, though. Tucked between a tailor and a travel agency or an ethnic grocery store, every empty storefront seemed to be an opportune place for a new culture-centric church to pop up.

Todd worked at an insurance agency and a few different churches as he continued to discern God's direction for his ministry. "I'd been in all monoethnic White churches, but my community wasn't monoethnic. My deep desire was to start a multiethnic church. But many leaders told me it could never happen. They told me that as a White minister, I'll never reach or lead anyone but White people. That kind of crushed what I felt God doing in my heart." He and his family have watched the process of "white flight"—families leaving our area as they've ceased to be the majority culture. Todd remembers sitting at his son's desk at parent-teacher night and realizing that his son was the only White kid in the classroom. Other White parents wondered why Todd and his wife, Jennifer, a Gwinnett County school teacher, hadn't asked for their son to be reassigned to another class. Others who had left for nearby counties wondered when the Jones family was finally going to give up and move out. Todd and Jennifer, however, have a vision beyond themselves and their White identities. Not only did they want to stay in their neighborhood and schools and keep their kids on their majority-minority sports teams, the Jones family longed for the diversity that they saw in the education system and the public square to finally permeate the church.

Todd kept asking himself if his vision was going to come from leaders with a narrow scope or if his vision was going to come straight from Jesus. Todd says we turn the Great Commission into the Great Omission when we stop at the "go . . . and make disciples" part. Too many of us forget to include the words, "of all nations." The paradigm of multicultural work in our denomination has been made up of predominantly segregated congregations existing in partnership with larger integrated denominational structures. If you ask about the work among "the nations" with most denominational members and leaders, they will respond with statistics of monocultural, often language-centric church plants and partnerships. While their heart certainly is for all nations to hear the good news and be discipled, they invest from a distance in ministries outside the context of their everyday lives.

Several years ago, we invited Todd to come serve in a temporary position as summer activities director at First Baptist Duluth. For two years, we had been trying to find the right fit for our vacant youth minister position. The more time we spent with Todd, the more we appreciated both his heart for God and for the people of our community. As he worked with our students and families, he began to recognize that the vision God had given him was the same vision God was working out in us. One night Todd had a dream in which he saw the faces of the youth before him. He awoke, then leaned over to his wife and whispered, "I think we're supposed to be at First Duluth." Soon, we approached him about becoming our interim and then our permanent youth minister. He now serves as student and family pastor for our congregation.

I persistently challenge our church members to live a "multicultural lifestyle." Who is allowed into your inner circle of relationships? Whom are you willing to share a meal with or invite to your home? Many people are idealistically multicultural. They know that limiting one's interactions to culture-centric relationships is not healthy and can come across as racist. And yet, they have not become practitioners of a multicultural lifestyle. The Jones family saw the peer group of their children as an opportunity to live out their multicultural values. Interactions at school, in sports, and everyday life were providing the open door for gospel conversations. Todd says, "If they don't have a relationship with Jesus, that's all the more reason we need to be in relationship with them." These ongoing interactions have made the Joneses' involvement in our multicultural church a natural extension of their everyday lives. Multicultural church leaders will never be truly effective until they are embracing a multicultural way of life.

Todd and his family stayed in Gwinnett County in order to follow God's call to lead in the multicultural church movement. But God is bringing this longing and vision to life in leaders from culture-centric churches, as well.

When I first met SoYoung Lee, a recent graduate from Southwestern Baptist Theological Seminary, she was serving as

ministry director for children at a Korean language church in the
Dallas/Fort Worth area. SoYoung and her husband, Kyung-Jong
(KJ), had come to the United States so that KJ could study at
the Medical College of Georgia in Augusta. During KJ's studies
in Augusta, Georgia, the family had attended a predominantly
White church in which they were the only Korean family. This
fellowship was 99 percent Anglo. KJ painfully recalls that some
members perpetuated racist White supremacist views that other
nationalities are not as blessed because of the "curse of Ham."
This perplexed immigrant family tried to understand how it
could be that American and English missionaries who carried
the gospel to their ancestors in Korea could have possibly come
from churches that considered them lesser beings. Upon his
graduation from medical school, KJ had taken a position as a
medical researcher in the metropolitan Dallas area. SoYoung and
KJ, along with their two daughters, Claire and Kaitlyn, moved to
Texas and made it their new home.

Upon arriving in Texas, the Lee family sought a church that
would meet their spiritual needs. Considering their previous
encounter, it is not surprising that they chose not to seek out a
White American church in their new location. The Lees were
initially delighted to learn of the numerous Korean churches
available to them in that area. They carefully chose a church that
provided them opportunities for exercising their spiritual gifts in
service. But soon after making their decision, KJ noticed the limitations of his new culture-centric Christian community. "I was
meeting people from many different nations and backgrounds in
my daily life but had no opportunity to share a worship experience with them. I wanted to invite many of my friends to church,

but there was no way they could feel at home since the whole service was conducted in Korean. We tried doing language interpretation, but it did not work." This experience caused the Lees to yearn for something different, something they had never seen, something they did not yet know even existed: a multicultural, multilingual community of faith.

The personnel search team at First Baptist Duluth asked SoYoung and her family to visit us and begin the prayer process to determine if she should serve on our ministry staff as preschool director. When I first met SoYoung, I shared with her my vision of creating a multicultural community of faith that could address the needs of our entire community, not just the portion that looked and talked like me. SoYoung was so overcome with this answer to her family's prayers that she began to weep with joy. When the family visited our morning worship service, they noticed Africans, Hispanics, Anglos, and Asians standing side by side in one setting. They said to one another, "This is what church should look like!" This was the type of Christian community God was giving them a vision for.

"If you don't see it before you see it, you will never see it," Dr. Johnny Hunt of the North American Mission Board once said. If we cannot picture the future, we cannot prepare for it. This principle is especially true of the type of leadership necessary for a multicultural congregation.

I have the great privilege of mentoring a pastor in Springdale, Arkansas. Billy Chidester's church sits in a diverse community with people originally from Laos, the Marshall Islands, Central and South America, and many other places. I guess you could say Billy has always had a heart for multicultural Christian fellowship, even in his marriage. Billy met his wife, Angelina, when they served together on a short-term mission in her hometown in Mexico. If you can believe it, when Billy and his wife were married, neither one of them was fluent in the other's language! That is commitment.

When Billy's church was facing some financial issues and changes in the congregation a few years ago, I suggested that he gather a vision team to help discern and orient the church to a central focus. I also suggested that, like our church, they should center on the primary mission of any church. Instead of bulldozing ahead as the visionary, Billy leaned into the people God had placed around him. He invited ten people to read through a book with him. Individually, each of them was to prayerfully choose three values they felt that the church should focus on. Billy said, "If we're all seeking Him, we're all going to be going in the same direction." As they completed the book and the group members came back together, each member of the group had chosen the same three points in the same order of priority. They saw God's hand in that. The vision was so Spirit-led and scriptural that when the committee shared the vision with the church, no one could argue with it! While multicultural ministry is valued in Billy's church, the vision team discerned that their central focus is being "a unified, praying church with Christ-centered worship, multiplying disciples in northwest Arkansas and the world." As we had concluded from our own experience developing a vision statement, the word *multicultural* doesn't need to be in the vision statement even if it is part of the heart of the church. The focus is on the Great Commission. If a church in a multicultural town or city is focused on reaching its community, it's inevitable that it's going to become a multicultural church, whether or not the word *multicultural* is written in the church's vision statement. As Thomas Hammond says, "Diversity is not the real win. Reaching a city with the gospel is the win." When Billy walked the vision discovery process with his Spirit-filled team, his leadership became more fruitful. Soon, second- and third-generation Hispanics began coming to the church and a family from Haiti joined. The church began to see greater diversity in the congregation without even trying.

Step Two: Devotion

When it comes to discerning a vision for ministry, too often leaders make a plan and then ask God to sign off on it. Even in our deacon, elder, or committee meetings, we often use prayer as a transition tool. Billy Chidester calls those "zipper prayers," one prayer to open a meeting and another to close it. As issues, concerns, or plans surface in meetings, Billy has learned to stop right then and there to ask God for His wisdom and leadership. But even when questions are lurking, Billy's prayers aren't primarily about problems, they are about God Himself! "Prayer should be worship-based, Scripture-fed, and Spirit-led," Billy says. "It's more about seeking God's face than it is about seeking His hand." He has learned that deep devotion and dependence starts with reverence, extolling God's holiness and omnipotence.

Zechariah 4:6 says: "'Not by strength or by might, but by my Spirit,' says the LORD of Armies." With that Scripture, the Holy Spirit convicted Billy that he had been relying on his own personal power to push forward a lot of things in the church. His modus operandi had been to trust in his own strength. Those efforts were being pruned away in his church's recent difficulties. I hear the humility in Billy's voice as we talk: "I had to quit leading in my own power and feel like I could just will it to be. I've seen what results I can get when I do things in my power. I want to see what happens when I'm fully submitted to the Spirit of God."

At First Baptist Duluth, we are attempting to develop a cultural intelligence that enables our members to effectively reach "all nations," because our community is comprised of "all nations." People often refuse to attempt cross-cultural interactions because they feel ill-equipped to do so. Pastor Todd Jones reminds us that "confidence comes from abiding." John 15:5 admonishes: "The one who remains in me and I in him produces much fruit, because you can do nothing without me." A great number of Christians are growing bad fruit or no fruit at all because they are not "abiding in Him."

When the church's leadership is abiding in Christ, seeking God's face in prayer and the Word, we can authentically invite our members to join us in deep devotion to Jesus, which goes hand in hand with a deep devotion to the church's vision of ministry.

When Thomas Hammond was pastor of First Baptist Alpharetta, he and his leadership team rolled out a huge map of their city. Over the next three months, groups from the church would walk every street praying over neighborhoods, families, businesses, and institutions. "You're going to see things while you're walking and praying that you wouldn't notice while you're driving," Pastor Hammond told his congregation. "So, when God places something on your heart, we want you to come back so we can talk about it." Each group adopted part of the city and highlighted the streets they prayer-walked each week. One group walked to an area two blocks from the church. In an alleyway that they'd never noticed from behind the steering wheel, they found a residential spot with eighteen Latino families. They prayed as they walked and came back to the church with the idea to offer tutoring for the children of those eighteen households during the school year.

Every Wednesday from 3:00 to 5:30, the group would tutor the children, feed them dinner at the church, and then give them the opportunity to go to kids' and middle school Bible study. The first week, two to three students came. The next week, five to six. The third week, around ten. Eventually, it was packed out. When Pastor Hammond peeked in the room where the ministry was taking place, the children's laughter and loud voices overtook the low volume of the hallway. He laughed and said to the leaders, "Good luck with all that!" As the leaders consistently spent time with these children, helping them and getting to know them as people, they were able to speak into their lives. Pastor Hammond overheard one senior adult sitting on the ground with an eight-year-old and saying, "God made you special and He has big plans for you." The leaders continued to devote themselves to prayer in the midst of their ongoing service. Every week the children's behavior and abilities were improving. Before God led this group to work with these students, some had not even known how to hold a pencil correctly!

After a couple of months, Pastor Hammond received a phone call. The lady on the line asked, "Are you the ones doing ministry with the kids on Marietta Street?" He said, "That depends—is this good news or bad news?!!" She said it was good news. "Oh, yes, that's us," he laughed. "I'm a teacher at the school," she said. "All the teachers and administrators are talking about how the kids have their homework done for the first time ever. They are more connected and focused, and their grades are going up." Pastor Hammond could hardly hold back his tears. Christmas was coming, so they planned a big celebration with the eighteen families. As members shared the gospel, eighteen adults prayed to receive Christ. Members walked the newcomers around the building and showed them the rooms where they could come for Bible study on Sunday morning with a bilingual elder named Bernardo. That sequence of events, starting with devoted prayer on the streets of the city, birthed the Spanish-speaking outreach of the church.

As leaders disciple our members into deeper communion with God, denominational leader Neal Eller says we'll find "it's no longer us doing the convincing." The Spirit of God leads all who are listening into deep compassion that presents almost like brokenheartedness. In recent years, God has given Neal and his wife, Cherri, a vision for welcoming international students from India into their home. Neal says he doesn't believe in "drive-by" missions. If they were going to do this, they were going to devote themselves to these students, making them a priority. If an event on the church or social schedule competed with their commitment to these students, they would choose the students every time. The original three students have become like adopted sons and daughters in their home. They even helped one of the students pick out her wedding dress. When they were invited to their student's Hindu wedding, they traveled all the way to India to be present in person for the celebration. As they visited the home-land of their beloved students, they felt God's deep love welling up and overflowing in them. Neal said, "I remember two separate times on our visit that my wife and I embraced one another and sobbed in each other's arms because we love the Indian people so much. We wept over the country and over the people groups who call it home. That had never happened to us before." As the couple has devoted themselves to prayer and service over the years, God has been expanding their capacity to love. We have experienced a similar sense of having our hearts deeply moved for our friends and neighbors as we've devoted ourselves to God and His call. Some believers view prayer as passive, yet prayer is how we fill up on God's love, discern specific strategies to try, and receive the energy we need to step forward and take action.

Step Three: Action

I often call our church's shift to multicultural ministry my Rubicon. I'm no king or warrior, but like Julius Caesar who led his army to the boundary between Italy and Gaul in 49 BC, there would be no turning back for me or my congregation. On that legendary day at the Rubicon River, it is reported that while leading his army into the water, Caesar shouted, *"Alea iacta est!"* which is translated: "The die is cast!" This phrase has become synonymous with a decision to press forward and not retreat, a "line in the sand," or a "point of no return." Every church attempting to transition to a multicultural model will eventually reach this critical junction where "the die is cast," the point in time when a return to past methodologies is no longer a legitimate option.

After discerning a vision and cultivating an ongoing devotion to the Giver of that vision, the time comes for us to act on what we know to be good and true.

When it came to our Korean friends, KJ and SoYoung Lee, their vision and devotion was clear, but their path was not. Although the Lees felt a strong desire to join the ministry and church family at First Baptist Duluth, KJ would need to find meaningful employment in the metro Atlanta area in order to make their transition possible. With the vast amount of medical facilities in proximity, we all felt certain that the prospect of Dr. KJ Lee securing a position to relocate his family to the area was merely a formality. Unfortunately, as months passed, this desire did not come to fruition. Month after month, every phone call we made to the Lee home in Dallas was the same. But still, SoYoung and KJ continued to reiterate their overwhelming sense of a call to be a part of the unique ministry at First Baptist Duluth.

As time drew near for the beginning of fall semester, the probability of having a position for KJ to relocate his family had grown dim. As their vision came up against their circumstance, they had to decide what to do. "Until then, I had followed wherever KJ went for a job or to study," SoYoung said. "We thought this was interesting that God may be leading us through my work and ministry, and if God would provide a job for KJ in Georgia, we would know this was God's will. But then it didn't happen. We both had to pray together and on our own to figure out what to do."

After much prayer and consideration, SoYoung and KJ called me with the news. The Lees were more certain than ever that they were called to be part of our ministry and leadership team. They had decided that even with the unknowns about KJ's work, SoYoung would come to Duluth with their two daughters, establish residence, and begin her work. KJ would stay in Dallas at his research post and continue his search for a position in the metro Atlanta area.

This long-distance living family situation was a sacrifice for this precious couple. Their dedication to the multicultural cause was noted by the church and motivated others to step up to meet needs. For two years, KJ traveled back and forth, working his job in Texas and being with his family in Georgia. As SoYoung helped the girls adjust to their studies and worked hard at leading in her new role, she kept hoping in the Lord. When she worried about how things were going to turn out, KJ always told her to go back to their calling. "You already crossed the river," he would say. As SoYoung stepped out and put her energy toward her calling, she became too busy to doubt!

Time went on and the research grant ran out for KJ's position in Dallas. When he moved to Duluth to join his family, it was the first time in his adult life that he had been without a job. But still, it was a significant moment for him. He saw that he could trust God in it. KJ eventually interviewed and accepted a position in the medical field in our area. SoYoung says her time as a working mother while KJ was living in another state gave her great empathy for the ongoing challenges that the single mothers in our preschool face.

The Lees' courage to take action and step forward before having all the pieces in place has benefited our community both spiritually, in the form of this unusual testimony of faith, and practically, in that we did not have to wait two years to add SoYoung's heart and expertise to our ministry staff. Many times, leaders must act before the structures are in place. A leader's action is dependent upon the call, not the challenges.

Thomas Hammond says, "This church was strong and they could've kept doing the same old same old, but they were brave and bold enough to say, 'Let's jump off of this worn path and create another.'" Leaders are informed by the past, but not stuck in it. They live and minister in the present, but they blend awareness with imagination to envision what could or should be and then act on it.

Hammond says, "There's more growing in the going than there ever will be sitting in the pew and listening. You're not going to grow until you get up and put into practice the principles or precepts you've been taught. We leaders have fed people to give them spiritual nutrition, but there can't be spiritual health without activity." As we saw in the perspectives of our legacy members, church is often the last bastion of "safety" for people who are afraid of the rapid changes of society. But according to Hammond, the church should be on the frontiers of change. Great explorers like Lewis and Clark were not afraid to go beyond the limits of the map. They were path makers, not just path followers. With Christ's mandate to go into all the world, our churches should be "marching off the map," leading the way in discussions of social and cultural issues.

Just as our vision and devotion are rooted in Jesus, so is our action. As SoYoung serves as preschool director, she disciples her staff to focus on Jesus. "I hope every one of us puts our eyes on the Lord and not our differences," SoYoung says. Former preschool workers who've returned to work since she came on staff have written letters saying that the environment is one of contentment and peace under her leadership. They say they love to come to work because they sense this is God's work.

KJ, who now serves as chairman of our deacons, says, "When I share the vision of our church with others, people think it is amazing!" KJ and SoYoung are proud that the church is leading the way with celebrating other cultures and embracing all people. But their greatest prayer is that the transformational gospel will go forth. As leaders broaden their vision, deepen their devotion, and step forward, churches will finally begin to address the entirety of the Great Commission that Jesus gave to the first disciples.

▼ ▼ ▼

CHAPTER EIGHT

God Has a Plan

Inclusion | Communication | Determination

"For I know the plans I have for you," declares the
LORD, "plans to prosper and not to harm you, plans
to give you hope and a future." (Jeremiah 29:11 NIV)

I find that doing the will of God leaves me no time
for disputing about his plan. (George MacDonald)

Jeremiah is the ultimate motivational speaker, acknowledging both the hardships of life and the sufficiency of God and His purposes. I have the words of Jeremiah 29:11–13 written on the first page of my prayer journal, and I quote this promise almost every day. Every believer needs to know that God has a plan and purpose for their life. This realization sustains me through difficult days and motivates me to accomplish His will for my life. The context of this passage is that the children of Israel have lived in captivity for seventy years. However, the prophet wants them to be encouraged that God is not finished with them.

Church leaders pursuing the path to doing church in technicolor will need to be firmly rooted in God's promises. Proper motivation is essential to ensure longevity and ultimate success. Assurance of God's will must be present in order to weather doubt, days of hard work, cross-cultural missteps, or vehement opposition. We cannot depend on people to comfort us when they are uncomfortable. We must take refuge in God and return refreshed to live out the vision He has given. I have advised our staff that every multicultural church leader needs to develop "the hide of a rhinoceros and the heart of a dove." The technicolor leader needs to be both compassionate and tenacious in pursuit of God's calling and plan.

Step Four: Inclusion

When we had a predominantly White congregation and leadership team, how could we expect our neighbors from other cultural and language backgrounds to find their way to us? We could reach out and build relationships in our everyday lives, but early on in our transition, if members invited friends from school or a sports team, newcomers to our congregation would not find the same diversity inside the doors of our building as they observed in the public square. It felt like a catch-22. We wanted more diverse neighbors to take part in our congregation, but we needed more diverse attenders in order for newcomers to want to come back. We quickly discerned that to help diverse visitors feel at home in the pew, we needed to put someone from their own language and culture on the platform. If we wanted to build bridges to different cultures and train the existing members to reach their neighbors, we were going to have to gather a diverse team of leaders. Our staff and leadership needed to change before the congregation ever could.

Knowing that a good percentage of our local population was Korean, we began looking for a Korean translator and interpreter. That search went on for three years until Tom (Jeong Doo) and Cindy (Seung-hee) Rhe and their three children found their way to Duluth. I became aware of the Rhe family through a Korean pastor in our state convention. When I saw on Facebook that they were moving to our area to complete Tom's seminary degree, I wondered if this might be our answer.

Someone has to be first in order for us to reach that new segment of our community. When Tom and Cindy and their three children came to First Baptist Duluth, they and the Lee family were the only two Korean families in the church. The Rhes and Lees were our outliers, our forerunners, representatives of some of the neighbors we wanted to reach. Cindy had worked as a Korean interpreter during the couple's college days. Prior to moving to the States, she had also served as a missionary for Operation Mobilization on the *Logos II* mission ship, an experience which afforded her the opportunity to visit forty different nations. God had uniquely prepared this lady for service in a multicultural church.

On a volunteer basis, Cindy began providing live Korean translation during the morning worship service. We found it humorous that when she first started, the only recipient of her interpretation ministry was her husband, Tom. But word quickly spread out in the community of the "American" church that was now open to Korean interaction. Within a year she was interpreting to about a dozen Korean friends. Today, there are about sixty Koreans regularly attending First Baptist Duluth.

At that same time, Tom joined our staff as an intern to help us begin connecting local Korean families to the church. During Tom's internship, he enlisted a retired Korean school principal to establish a cultural center offering more than twenty classes for writing, art, music, and sports. Twice a week, on Thursdays and Saturdays, neighbors enter our church building or meet on the soccer field, cultivating their skills and connecting with the congregation. As Tom finished his internship, his wife, Cindy, became an intern herself, formally taking leadership of our language ministry.

After her eighteen-month internship, Cindy accepted a part-time position on our staff. As she observed the ministries we currently had going, she felt compelled to start morning English as a Second Language (ESL) classes to complement our existing evening ESL program. She recruited teachers and other volunteers and has grown the Wednesday-morning program to more than fifty students from twenty-four countries. The position and need continued to grow, so we were grateful to have Cindy come on full-time as One Voice Language Ministry coordinator in 2020. Cindy's work has many facets. She oversees live interpretation in three languages—Korean, Spanish, and Mandarin—and helps translate documents to help us better communicate with our Korean members and visitors. She coordinates the distribution of Bibles in more than twenty-five languages, and she assists with the largest English institute in the county as our volunteers teach English to more than three hundred participants. God knew the type of person that we would need to reach our multilingual community, and He provided a wonderful resource in sending us Cindy.

Cindy says one of the ways she sees God using her as a leader is in her humility and authenticity. She enjoys being an example for her students, demonstrating that leaders do not have to have everything figured out in order to contribute. "The students watch these native-speaker English teachers working with me, a broken-English-speaking Korean lady, as their director," Cindy says. "They see that I lead our team of American teachers, and that those teachers love working with me. I like being a role model encouraging these students that anyone can get involved and become a leader even if their English is not perfect." Cindy is learning as she goes, just like them. This shows the students that they don't need to hide their customs or their accent. With people like Cindy on our team and as White American members follow her leadership, visitors can also see there is no room for feelings of superiority or inferiority in our community. Leadership is not limited by language, color, or culture.

Cindy's Korean name is a compound Korean word: *Seung* means "connections," and *Hee* means "girl." Therefore, her name literally means "connections girl." Her name describes her natural gifting and the scope of her ministry. "I'm living out my name," she says with excitement. "This is my gift from God. He made me good at connecting people with Jesus and connecting people with people. I can see each person's gifts and connect them with where they need to be. And through interpreting and translation,

I can connect people from many languages and help them become involved in the life of the church." Cindy is connecting our diverse congregation with God, with culture, and with language that helps them in their everyday life. Adding Tom and Cindy to our church family and staff team has helped us to get to know the Korean culture and has helped people from the Korean culture to get to know us.

Similarly, ministry intern Charlotte Kumar expanded our reach with South Asian visitors and neighbors. Charlotte felt like part of our church family even before she had set foot on American soil. Her brother Kadmiel serves as a deacon at our church and her oldest brother, Daniel, is lead pastor for Good News Centre, one of our partner ministries in Delhi, India. Charlotte graduated from Bible college in India, and shortly thereafter, as part of her cultural tradition, she was promised in an arranged marriage with an Indian pastor. Sadly, the marriage was unhealthy, and the Kumar family eventually learned that Charlotte was trapped in an abusive relationship and an unsafe environment. She found herself praying, "God, I have lost everything. I have lost my family, my husband, my house, and my dignity in society." Charlotte says, "If you are divorced or a widow in India, it's as if you don't exist. After escaping the abuse at home, you then get a lot of abuse from society. You are an outcast." Her parents took her in, not wanting her to live in a situation where she felt as if she were dying every day. The family agreed that divorce was the best option for Charlotte's safety and well-being, but as divorce is not culturally accepted in India, they felt that Charlotte needed a fresh start in life. She and her brothers discussed some possibilities and determined that Charlotte should move to the United States to begin a doctorate program in missions at New Orleans Baptist Theological Seminary. The seminary required a one-year waiting period after her legal divorce, along with documented evidence of her receiving proper spiritual counseling.

After a period of emotional and spiritual recovery, Charlotte enrolled in seminary and journeyed to the States to begin her own studies. She lived with her brother Kadmiel and served as a seminary intern at our church during her doctoral studies. As global ministry intern, she spent her time building relationships with ESL families and planning international events. She shared the gospel with many students through the ESL program. One Pakistani Muslim friend from ESL started coming to church on Sundays and asking questions of spiritual significance.

Charlotte also served for a season as the family ministry intern, helping with children and preschool ministry. She greeted families and developed friendships with many Indian parents. "In true Indian style, I would invite myself to their house and say, 'I'm missing some chai. I'm missing some Indian food.' They were especially honored when I brought Pastor Mark's wife, Glenda, with me." Charlotte, Glenda, and other friends would visit many houses together and take gifts, groceries from the church, and a New Testament in the family's language. They would talk about their festivals and their interests. As each friendship grew, Charlotte would ask if she and other church members could pray for them and would explain why they pray in Jesus' name. On the next visit, the people would say, "I think prayer works," and give testimony of the surprising way a prayer was answered.

As she devoted herself to incarnational ministry, Charlotte worked diligently to write a dissertation on equipping churches to care for Hindu people. Including a Spirit-filled leader like Charlotte on our ministry team has allowed our church to expand our ministry beyond our walls and develop resources that will bless other churches and their Hindu neighbors. Her personable nature and cultural competency have given other leaders and members at the church a certain credibility and familiarity in the eyes of our South Asian neighbors in particular. Her bold intentionality has also modeled for us White American leaders and members how natural it can be to enter the circles of our neighbors and show our care for them.

Reflecting on her experience serving on a staff with so many different backgrounds, Charlotte says, "It was unique. People brought their culture to the table. We worked together even though we were from different places. We knew our personal goals, and we were working towards one common goal. Pastor Mark makes everyone feel that they are an equal member of the team. Korean, Nigerian, Indian—everybody at the table is important. Everyone has potential. He was confident about the talent God has given us. He challenged us to grow." After surviving emotional and physical abuse, Charlotte marvels at how God healed her and raised her up again to do kingdom work both in India and in metro Atlanta.

Our interns and other international staff members bring a wealth of hands-on ministry perspectives from their countries of origin as well as provide insights into their immigrant experience for the White Americans on the team. As transformational churches begin to include leaders from all nations on their church staff, opportunities to connect new diverse neighbors to the local church will greatly increase.

"I see it as the spirit of inclusive representation," says Abioye Tela, our local ministry intern from Nigeria. "This church brought me to study and be on staff here in order to advertise to the world that we are doing multiethnic ministry. I'm included because this is the heart of the church. In the few years I've been here, Pastor Mark has released the pulpit and allowed me to preach several times. That's rare in ministry. Very, very rare. The most recent time I preached, he was sitting in the congregation. He was not on leave. He was not on vacation. I was not a fill-in. He sat down to listen to the Word under my leadership. If I'm to remember anything about the last decade, that is going to stand out. He has also invited me to administer the Lord's Supper and given me the privilege of leading baptism. These things have boosted acceptance of my culture by the congregation. This is what we believe. This is what we live out. We can work and worship together." As members see the faces, hear the voices, and witness the influence and leadership of staff members from Korean, Indian, African, and other backgrounds, legacy members become more comfortable with our multicultural vision and newcomers from other language and cultural backgrounds feel more at home in our sanctuary.

Step Five: Communication

No matter how strong the leadership is, the transition to multicultural ministry will bring about periods of instability in the church. During this time, it is vital that the leadership team be ready to communicate the vision and the strategies repeatedly with clarity and offer a patient, listening ear as members

get accustomed to the changes. Members had been wringing
their hands saying, "Something needs to be done." Now, we are
pursuing a positive direction with a profound message to address
a perplexing circumstance. People may not feel totally at ease
with where we are heading as a church, but everyone knows the
direction and the biblical reasoning behind it. In staff meetings,
church business meetings, and sermons, we spent months communicating the "why" and not just the "what" of the upcoming
changes. We spent a great deal of time readying families for next-
generation ministries that will no longer have a majority culture.
We also communicated practical information including the likelihood of a shortfall in budget receipts as some families would
flee the diversifying community and giving would drop. The
community changed rapidly, and now, with ongoing thoughtful
communication, the church is adjusting at increased velocity and
improving attitude.

Part of the change has come from the humble, compassionate
communication of our staff members as disappointed members
approach them with issues to discuss. When things begin to
change within a church, people who have been there long-term
may only notice the change and not notice those things that have
remained consistent. This has proven true repeatedly in the arena
of music. Some congregants only want to sing the "old songs." As
we began to introduce new choruses in different languages, they
would stop singing out. Critics would occasionally come to our
music directors and express their longing for the "good old days,"
those hymns that "we all know." On one such encounter, one of
our music leaders said, "Let's look at this together." He calmly
and patiently took out the previous week's worship planning

sheet and allowed the concerned member to look over the order of worship. As the member scanned the list, they realized that we had sung three hymns that Sunday. The reality is that some things have changed, but much has remained. Years ago, a multicultural church consultant advised us to transition our church away from including choir and orchestra in our worship services. But in honor of the roots of our legacy members, we chose to keep traditional elements of worship within the church and blend them with ethnic celebrations. We continue to have a choir and an orchestra, but it is not your typical traditional service. It is a beautiful blend of Asian, African, Latino, and American expressions that reflect our congregation.

Mark Barneycastle, our worship pastor and Global Ministry coordinator, says as we continue to grow, he envisions gathering a diverse group of voices to speak into what the church's worship services should look like and sound like. Mark first experienced multilingual worship on a mission trip to Chile. Although this was a profound stretch from his upbringing, he testifies that leading worship in a multicultural setting "felt like what I had been looking for all my life." Mark has a heart for diverse music and trusts himself to include a wide variety of music in our services, but he also acknowledges that even open-minded people may have things they're overlooking. Good communication involves opening the conversation to hear back from those who are affected by leadership decisions. Expanding to a multicultural worship service may be very painful for people who love traditional American church music. If you're changing your music style and content, that transition is probably going to be met with more resistance than any other transition since music is so connected to the heart. Mark says, "If people aren't worshiping in their heart music, they will see worshiping outside their heart music as not feeling worshipful, whether it's multicultural or not."

Coming from a more contemporary musical background, Mark was less familiar with choir and orchestra and many of the hymns, something that many of our legacy members found rather shocking. Many people fought against what they perceived as a steady drift toward full-on contemporary style led by this bearded, acoustic guitar-carrying twenty-something with jeans and an untucked shirt. One Easter, Mark planned three hymns for the worship service and felt he was coming through for the traditional folks, but the feedback told him that he didn't sing the "right" hymns, the "Easter hymns." There was one church member, one who usually approaches Mark with a blend of straight-forwardness and encouragement, who texted Mark at 4:30 in the morning about how heartbroken he was that they didn't sing "Up from the Grave He Arose." When Mark woke up and read the message, his first instinct was frustration, but then he stopped and thought about things from this person's perspective, how that might have been the first Easter in that person's life that he hadn't sung that particular hymn at church.

A couple of years ago when Mark was struggling, he shared his concerns with a worship leader friend. That worship leader asked, "Are you stretching yourself to learn new things just as you're asking the worship team and congregation to learn new things?" Mark replied, "Absolutely. I'm stretching like crazy. I'm learning a ton of hymns, learning about new instruments, learning other ways of leading worship." And then the worship leader asked, "Do your people know that?" Mark paused and said, "I don't think so." Mark has learned the importance of allowing the legacy members to see that he, too, is stretching, learning, and growing. As leaders, we can communicate from example as well as with words. After that epiphany, Mark decided to be more vulnerable and let people see just how much he was stretching himself.

Before leading a hymn that many of them had been singing "since nine months before they were born," he would humbly tell the congregation, "This is a new one for me. I just learned it last week. I really fell in love with the rich words of this song as I've been singing it in preparation for today's service." He discovered that after our more traditional members got over the initial shock of learning that he didn't know "Have Thine Own Way" or "Down at the Cross," they would approach him and say, "Thank you for learning these hymns. It means a lot to us." In this humble, honest communication, Mark empathizes and lets our congregants know he is feeling some of the growing pains with them as he leans toward their habits and preferences and releases some of his.

Mark says his time on staff has helped him grow to appreciate even the less-than-flattering communication from church members. "Listen to negative people," he says. "They may stay negative, but you can still learn from them. Don't just wish them away. Engage. We don't need to get along all the time. I've found that the people who make life more difficult for me in some ways also make life better. Peace doesn't mean the absence of conflict." Conflict with good communication can actually be a catalyst for spiritual and emotional growth. Interestingly, our work with people from other languages and ethnicities can give us patience for the cultural divides with the people who look the most like us. This will make us better communicators. When the differences are more obvious, our approach tends to be more intentional. Abioye Tela says, "The way someone talks. It is not wrong. It is not stupid. The way someone smells. It is not wrong. It is not stupid. The way someone dances. It is not wrong. It is not stupid. You are from a different culture. I am from a different culture. I will surprise you. You will also surprise me. But I will not intentionally offend you. Let's forgive in advance." With humble, compassionate communication, we can prepare our congregations for change and comfort them when that change is painful.

Step Six: Determination

Mark Barneycastle had been drawn to the idea of multicultural church for many years, but he was still not sure of its long-term viability. Ministry is already difficult. What kind of leader would sign up to deal with apprehension from existing church members, encounter many awkward moments in cross-cultural relationships, and endure the fiery darts of the enemy as we approach long-standing spiritual strongholds? Mark came into this opportunity with a bit of trepidation. He wanted to make sure that he wasn't going to take on the stress of a position like this only to watch it all come to nothing. Before he came on staff, Mark sat down with me and asked, "Is failure an option?"

He was sold on the vision and call, and I assured him of my determination. But still, he wasn't sure that the entire leadership team and church membership were committed and ready to persevere. Was this just a last-ditch effort to keep the church from

dying? Or were our people passionate about the call and ready
to persevere even when things became difficult? We gave the
Barneycastles enough evidence of our commitment, and Mark
came to serve with us first as an intern in 2016, then as interim
worship leader in 2017, and then full-time on pastoral staff in 2019.
"It was an open door and we walked through it," Mark says. "I was
confident at least in Pastor Mark and Glenda's commitment to the
multicultural vision for the church. Now that we're here, we're here
for more than Mark and Glenda. We have seen the congregation
live out many of the ideals that my family wanted in a multicultural
church. This church is committed to do whatever it takes to see
the vision come to fruition. Since that time of decision, God has
continually confirmed that this is where He has called our family."
Like the rest of us, Mark has had to do his work within the tension of transition. Some business meetings were so unpleasant that
Mark wanted to hide under a table or find the side door and slip
out. He said, "During my first year at the church, I often asked
myself the question: Is there an easier option?" His conclusion was
that being where God wanted him to be, doing what God wanted
him to do, was the best option—easy or not! Mark says, "There
are times when it is a blast. This is by far the best job I have ever
had . . . but it's also the most difficult one."

It is difficult because we're not just dealing with the messiness
of interpersonal communication and mere human disagreement.
We're dealing with spiritual forces that don't want to see the good
news go out to all nations. Mark says, "We are coming up on some
strongholds of the enemy that aren't going to come down easily.
They're going to come down, but not easily." Mark emphasizes
that, for a leader, this kind of heavy lifting requires special care.

Leaders will run themselves into the ground if they're not careful. It's important to slow down and recharge. An investment in emotional and physical health is an investment in the ministry. "Ministry is hard. Multicultural ministry is even harder," he says. "If you let it, it will affect you." As we seek to work long-term, it is important to heed the call not just to ministry, but to Sabbath rest. Along with taking a weekly day of quiet restoration with his family, Mark has put some daily practices in place to help strengthen his spirit for the work here. He takes time to pray and do Scripture reading in the tradition of the Daily Office each day, waking up to communion with God in the morning, taking a break for meaningful connection midday, pausing to acknowledge God's presence and leading as the work day ends, and looking back on his day with God as he heads to bed each night. These check-ins throughout the day allow this leader's spirit to be nourished by God so he can sustain his energy in ministry and discern the needs of others around him. "We're transitioning a 135-year-old church. We have a chance to lay a foundation for another 135 years if Jesus doesn't return before then," Mark says. "I want this ministry to last, but it needs to be sustainable long-term. If you're moving too fast, you miss people and you overlook injustices. I can't invest in the vision and do good ministry for the people in my care if I'm not well. Will I sacrifice my comfort? Absolutely. But I'm not sacrificing my well-being or my family's well-being on the altar of church or ministry. There are some costs God doesn't call us to pay."

A great example of the determination needed to accomplish technicolor ministry is the story of my neighboring pastor friend Tito Ruiz. Tito is a native of Nicaragua. The northeast part of

Nicaragua was colonized by England and is mostly African descent. The black population there speaks English and other dialects but very little Spanish. The southwest part of Nicaragua was colonized by Spain, so you see more Whites with Spanish as the main language, no dialects. Tito is a mixture of African and Spanish: mestizo. He feels that God prepared him for multicultural ministry even in his DNA.

When he first came to the United States as a young adult, Tito played piano for a ministry—bringing concerts and gospel presentations to local apartment complexes where people from many languages and ethnicities lived. Tito attended a church where there were seven different churches of different language backgrounds meeting in the same building at different times. Quarterly, they had a combined service where people would pray in Mandarin, Spanish, and various languages and dialects. Tito found it beautiful. From the beginning of his time in the United States, he had been involved in multiethnic experiences, so he assumed this was the norm in our country. As time went on, he discovered the many inequities in our country's history and present day. When God called Tito to ministry, it was a deep conviction of his that he would not pastor a monolingual church. His vision was to pastor not a Spanish-speaking church or an English-speaking church, but a bilingual church where both languages and cultures had full expression. God was calling him to break the walls of culture and language and make the multicultural model as normal as Tito thought it was when he first set foot on American soil. "I don't know if I was being naive," Tito says, "but little did I know how hard that was going to be."

Tito was asked to launch a Spanish-speaking congregation at an English-speaking church in our county. It wasn't the multicultural ministry he dreamed of leading, but it was a step in the right direction. As Tito began leading his small congregation in the middle of a predominantly White church, there was opposition from the first moment to the last. Tito's congregation had the support and friendship of the lead pastor, but the pastor's staff and leaders were not in agreement. His Spanish-speaking congregation often felt under attack by their mother church. There was territorialism with the shared space in the student center. Efforts to fellowship were met with unease. Often minority ministries being hosted at predominantly White churches are treated like outsiders or even second-class citizens. "There are rooms that are locked. 'Don't touch this. Don't use that. Don't go in there. That's mine. That's ours.' That has been my experience of ministry in the United States," Tito says.

Tito's strong relationship with the lead pastor kept him focused and encouraged during these days of complaints and cold-shoulder attitudes. Periodically, the two congregations would worship together. *Now, this is how the church should worship*, Tito thought. Tito recalls preaching a sermon together with his mentor. Tito preached in fluent English and the lead pastor read his sermon in Spanish, which he had never done before. This tremendous attempt to preach in unity was met with outrage from a segment of the congregation. One disgruntled member emailed the lead pastor: "I come to church to learn about God. If I want to learn Spanish, I'll go to Mexico!" To no one's surprise, this church is no longer in existence. Sadly, the demise of the mother church left Tito and his congregation "homeless." Tito's congregation found a home at another English-speaking church. As a new pastor transitioned in, he told Tito, "I have no idea what to do with a Spanish-speaking ministry." He saw the group as a separate entity and told them he had to let them go. Tito prayed, "Okay, Lord, what do we do?"

These disappointments would take time to process, but I am amazed at the gentleness and joy that Tito exudes even after being treated so cavalierly. He chooses to turn away from focusing on the sin of the person and turn toward what God is doing in the situation. Tito trusts that even with the ungodly decisions some leaders are making, God is still at work. Tito, who loves to spend time in the kitchen creating new recipes, says, "Okay, Lord, when You cook, it's going to be something delicious. The ingredients by themselves taste ugly. We don't want to eat spices on their own. You're putting it all together. Lord, You have a bigger plan. You are all over this."

God has used imagery from the Bible to make it so that Tito doesn't become bitter or hold on to resentment. As Tito reflects on the injustice he and his congregation have received, he considers the healing of the commander, Naaman. In the story, it was the slave of the commander's wife who gave the suggestion that Naaman go to the prophet and ask to be healed. "This is a girl who should have been wishing for her master to die. And the moment he dies, maybe she has a chance to get out of there," Tito says. "Yet, she blessed him." With this attitude of focusing on the well-being of even those leaders who are hard-hearted, Tito is able to forgive and bless those who've overlooked or mistreated him and his congregation. Despite everything, Tito remains in a good relationship with all the previous pastors he's worked with.

Tito's wife, a scientist for the Center for Disease Control in Atlanta, took a business trip to Italy, where she discovered a blended congregation that worshiped in both Spanish and Italian. Tito already had a passion for bilingual worship and preaching. His wife's experience in Italy reminded him of his desire to pastor a multicultural congregation. Having his congregation dismissed from churches again and again, Tito decided that from this time forward, his congregation would be bilingual with shared leadership from both Latinos and Anglos. He would teach his congregation: "We are more alike than different through the Word of God."

As he sought guidance from friends, one local megachurch pastor said, "In order for a multiethnic church to work, it needs to be led by a White pastor." He told Tito he knew that sounded terrible, but he genuinely believed that most Whites would not submit to the leadership of a minority. Tito was speechless at first. As he considered all he had learned about ethnic tension in the United States, he wondered if his friend might be right. But who are we to argue with the call God has put on someone's life and ministry, even if our dominant culture resists it? Tito says, "The megachurch mentality is always about how to grow your church with the wow factor, but my definition of ministry success is to be obedient to what I'm called to do. I'm called to have a strong Christ-centered forever-lasting marriage. I'm called to disciple my family. And I'm called to pastor a congregation that breaks down the walls of language and culture."

Tito would need that clarity and determination as he branched off and started his own church. The church initially rented space adjacent to our building, making them our nearest neighbor.

Tito preaches in Spanish and then interprets each section of his sermon in English. Guest speakers start in one language, and a live interpreter communicates in the other language. A lot of the church's families are culturally mixed. One spouse may speak more Spanish than English or vice versa. There are members of European descent, Latin Americans, African Americans, and couples with one Latino and one White or one African American and one White. It is a welcome place for many, but the work of building his congregation has not been a Utopia. Some Latinos left because English was now spoken in their services. Some English speakers have steered away from the congregation because Spanish is spoken there. It has been difficult to find a consistent space to meet. It can be discouraging to think that Tito and his people have been together more than a decade and are still "homeless." But through these challenges, Tito has been shaped and has developed a new way of measuring success. Tito says, "There is a big difference between a calling and a job. If you are only in it for the paycheck, when things get tough, you will move to another job. God didn't call me to get certain results or present my 'return on investment.' When you are called, the metrics measured are less about success and more about obedience."

The everyday work is the living out of the calling. It isn't based on human estimation. Tito has received many invitations from White pastors to interview for a role as Spanish-speaking pastor, but the conviction to build a truly multicultural church is so strong that saying no to those offers has not been a challenge.

North American Mission Board Vice President Kim Robinson says that he has seen pastors of predominantly White churches get terminated simply for inviting a Hispanic family to the church.

On one occasion, a deacon walked into the pastor's office and told him there had been a vote and he was out. That pastor was married and had four children in the local school system. The church's decision upended the work of God and this family's well-being. Fear about this type of reaction has stopped many ministers from attempting what they sensed was best for their church and for the community. Tito admires the determination of First Baptist Duluth's leaders, how we are not seeking to please any one culture, but to follow the conviction of God. "It's a big deal to know there are courageous people out there," says Tito. "There's a bigger kingdom out there beyond the issues within the four walls, or no walls, of my church."

Hugh Townsend, a retired pastor and denominational leader, recounts a previous ministry marked by disappointment. Earlier in his ministry, his congregation turned down his vision to reach out to the African American community literally on the other side of the tracks from them in his town in Maryland. Later in his ministry, local church leaders in another area ignored the importance of prayer initiatives and made programming their priority. Disappointed or not, God's call remains the same and it's only going to be lived out in us when we are dependent on Him and not on the reactions of those around us. Hugh says, because of our perseverance, First Baptist Duluth stands as an example of how to work through the muddy waters even when there are some members who are not excited about it.

Multicultural ministry is hard. We come up against fear, misunderstandings, and a lot of extra work that you won't find in a monocultural church. But as Hebrews 10:36–38 (NIV) says: "You need to persevere so that when you have done the will of God, you will receive what he has promised. For, 'In just a little while, he who is coming will come and will not delay.' And, 'But my righteous one will live by faith. And I take no pleasure in the one who shrinks back.'"

Multicultural church rarely feels easy, yet surprisingly, it often feels joyful. Our determination is fueled by God's calling and strength, confidence in His plan, and the satisfaction of seeing His promises come to fruition in front of us. Looking back on the difficulties of cross-cultural ministry, Tito says confidently, "When we are called and things get tough, the same God who called us will sustain us." I agree. Calling does not have to give way when opposition comes. Challenges can lead us into deeper dependence on God and each other, which makes us even stronger than we were before.

CHAPTER NINE

▼ ▼ ▼

I Have a Dream!

Reconciliation / Collaboration / Education

Everything is from God, who has reconciled us to himself through Christ and has given us the ministry of reconciliation. (2 Corinthians 5:18)

Some men see things the way they are and ask, "Why?" I dream of the way things could be and ask, "Why not?" (George Bernard Shaw)

On August 23, 1963, Rev. Martin Luther King Jr. stood at the foot of the Lincoln Memorial in Washington, DC, and gave his most famous speech. His "I Have a Dream" speech has been studied by students for decades. The repeated refrain has become the rallying cry for racial unity and reconciliation for a generation.

I have a dream . . .

    That one day on the red hills of Georgia the sons of slaves and the sons of former slave owners will be able to sit down together at the table of brotherhood.

I have a dream . . .

    That one day even in the state of Mississippi, a state sweltering with the heat of injustice . . . will be transformed into an oasis of freedom and justice.

I have a dream . . .

    That my four little children will one day live in a nation where they will not be judged by the color of their skin, but by the content of their character.

I have a dream today!

When I first shared my heart for developing a multicultural church with colleagues and fellow ministers, I was repeatedly reminded of the enormity of the task and chastised that my dream of bringing ethnicities and cultures into a single community of faith is an "impossible task." But I believe in BIG dreams. God wants us to dream big dreams so He can show Himself as a BIG GOD.

I knew the First Baptist Duluth needed an "I have a dream" moment, a clarion call of commitment to unifying all ethnicities into a singular family of faith. The apostle Peter had a similar calling on the Day of Pentecost in Acts 2. Peter had denied knowing Jesus three times on the morning of the Lord's crucifixion.

However, in Acts, he delivered the first public sermon in the newly founded Jerusalem church on a most auspicious occasion. A miracle had just occurred that enabled everyone present to hear the gospel in their native language. Some were amazed, but many were fearful of the meaning of this phenomenal event. This prompted the apostle to share his dream of what the infant church would look like and ultimately accomplish. Since the first century, the Christian church has struggled with equality, acceptance, and inclusion. Peter said in his sermon: "Your young men will see visions, and your old men will dream dreams" (Acts 2:17). I heard one preacher say that "young men" filled with God's Spirit are not afraid of the future. I love seeing millennial leaders who approach issues with tenacity that God is going to be ultimately victorious. On the other hand, "older men" controlled by the Spirit are not afraid to die. They know their final destiny. Therefore, they have the courage to abandon themselves to God's plan once it is discovered. I so admire those in our church who are twenty years my senior and yet continue to look and lead into the future. I am getting closer to their chapter of life and I want to emulate their faithfulness to God's plan.

Step Seven: Reconciliation

In recent years, I have become close friends with Kim Robinson, a former vice president of the North American Mission Board. Kim is a former executive with Proctor & Gamble Corporation. Kim moved to Atlanta in retirement to be near children and grandchildren. He went to the NAMB offices in nearby Alpharetta to offer his services as a volunteer. Within months, he was hired on a contract basis and in less than three months he became a special assistant to the president of the mission board. Kim is an African American with a rich and varied background in church life. He shared with me about a time in his career when he and his family moved to Boston. They began their search for a church home. Kim had previously been involved both in predominantly White congregations and in predominantly African American congregations. He and his wife, Tammy, had determined that their new church search would not be based upon skin color. On Sunday morning he led his family to the first church in their search process. As they settled into a pew, they immediately recognized that they were the only people of color in the room. His family felt the uncomfortable stares of regular parishioners. Kim and Tammy whispered to one another that they would stay through the service but would hightail it out of there as soon as the last hymn was sung. As the Robinsons made their way through the doors of the auditorium, the pastor ran to greet them. "We're glad you worshiped with us today," the pastor said, "but I think you may have come to the wrong service. There's a Black church that meets after us at one o'clock." Kim was disappointed to hear of this intentional segregation of the church. Kim says, "For a lot of people, their mindset is that we don't fellowship together. They're going to be pretty surprised in heaven when every ethnicity and language is going to be represented." This experience had a profound effect upon Kim and Tammy, propelling them to be passionate advocates for multicultural churches.

There have been times when I have been accused of being one dimensional in my approach to ministry. Some people have said I speak too much about diversity. Some people have grumbled.

Some people have stopped attending worship services with us. Some have even stopped giving. It can be discouraging as a leader to share a God-given message again and again and still see people who just "don't get it." Kim Robinson says he often tires of educating people as to what it is like to be Black in America. This dear African American brother graciously awaits opportunities to share his minority experience with people who seldom ask his opinion. God has called the church to a ministry of reconciliation. Therefore, whatever our background, as leaders we cannot put a limit on how many times we are to preach out of a heart for unity, seeking to resolve inequities.

Kim is afraid that too many Christians are getting their worldview from the national news outlets rather than solid exegesis of the Word of God. Therefore, people quickly become labeled and their message diminished. Buzz phrases like "social gospel" and "woke theology" have emphasized the divide that remains in the American church. Reconciliation is an ongoing process that demands the energy and attention of leaders who care about the future of the church. Our worship pastor, Mark Barneycastle, is a White millennial reared in a rather homogeneous setting, and yet, he is passionate about the church recognizing inequalities and systemic injustices. Mark notes, "People of color are easily marginalized even in authentically diverse communities when their voice and perspective does not match up with what the majority culture deems normal."

The Bible teaches that loving our "brother" is a mark of genuine faith (1 John 4:20). Kim serves in his church on the parking lot team. This former Fortune 500 executive can be seen weekly directing traffic at his local church. The team of volunteers is mostly men who are fifty to sixty-five years of age, primarily blue-collar workers, and for the most part, politically conservative. Recently, Kim's pastor was addressing a difficult sermon on race. He asked Kim to preface the sermon with a word of testimony. Kim spoke at the beginning of the message and then returned to the back of the auditorium to join his team of parking lot servants. Not many of his coworkers knew that Kim had been an executive in a major company, nor did they know the struggle that he and his family had dealt with him being a Black leader in a predominantly White man's world. Kim's ongoing relationship serving alongside these men in the parking lot ministry has opened scores of opportunities for him to answer questions and expand his peers' perspectives.

Kim says, "In corporate America I can expect respect and care in cross-cultural interactions. Why should one expect anything less from the church?" I firmly believe with the diversification of America, churches that refuse to become as colorful as their communities will find themselves irrelevant in a rapidly changing world. Integration of every segment of society has come with challenges and opposition, but failure to involve the church in this process will greatly cripple the work of the gospel. Oftentimes Kim will say, "When you count others as more important than yourself, that is when the gospel is about to break through."

Step Eight: Collaboration

A few years ago, I noticed a large migration of African families moving to our community and securing health-care jobs, including my beloved neighbors, a Nigerian woman who is an anesthesiologist and her husband who pastors an African church. When our staff began to pray about how we could embrace the African segment of our community, I sought the advice of my friend and adviser Danny McCain, a missionary and professor who lives and works in Nigeria. I learned that Dr. McCain was at that time working as an editor on an African Study Bible. This new Bible is based on the New Living Translation and has notes written by 343 African church leaders from forty-three different African countries representing dozens of different denominations. As the project neared completion and publication, the publisher began to plan dedication services across the continent of Africa to celebrate this historic accomplishment. The publisher also wanted to bring this new Bible to the United States to serve the diaspora of Africans who now call America home. Plans were underway to have a dedication service in Chicago, the home office of the publisher. Knowing our church's demographics and direction in ministry, Danny wondered if we might be interested in hosting a similar event in Duluth. He could not think of anyplace more suited for introducing this helpful resource to the United States. We hardly had to think about it. We enthusiastically accepted, and soon we were making plans to host a launch party debuting the new African Study Bible to our community. African singers, dancers, and preachers came from as far away as Birmingham to participate in the event. Danny was greatly appreciative of the efforts and saw this event as a watershed moment in our church's desire to reach out to the African portion of our community. Danny says, "Now, when I return from the mission field to First Baptist Duluth, I greet people from Nigeria, Ghana, Liberia,

Togo, Malawi, Uganda, Ethiopia, and other parts of Africa. This is a different kind of church."

Georgia Baptist Executive Thomas Hammond laments that old structures within denominations have traditionally provided minority leadership roles only for catalysts that aided the denomination to reach their specific people group. However, new structures need to be established that provide minority leadership across the gamut of decision making and strategic planning. First Baptist Duluth intern Abioye Tela applauds our church for being on the cutting edge of this transformation in leadership approach. Upon arriving at First Baptist Duluth, Abioye noticed the shared leadership model at the church where the staff was comprised of Africans, Koreans, Hispanics, and Indians, as well as Americans. Pastor Tela also rejoiced that the church regularly observed cultural holidays that embraced the many different ethnicities within the community. However, he was most impressed with the shared planning of these events with ethnic leaders from both within the church and in the community. In 2018, when the church established "African Unity Day," Abioye, as the first African-born staff member, took the lead in planning the event along with a diverse group of African members and attenders. Abioye and other members from African backgrounds have led us non-Africans in loosening up, even dancing down the aisles for the offering time on our Celebrate Africa Sunday to demonstrate how God loves a cheerful giver, or celebrating the names of God to the beat of an African talking drum, the same type of drum used to welcome royalty in African nations. The procession ended with all in attendance joining in the familiar words of the old hymn "All Hail the Power of Jesus Name" set to a tune used in many African churches. Since the time that Abioye and friends introduced their authentic cultural celebrations into our congregation, the church has elected two African men to serve on the deacon body and several families have become involved in various forms of church leadership. Collaboration is the key to forming leadership relationships that work!

The journey into technicolor ministry does not always necessitate creating new paths. At times, it will take us to previous ministry initiatives that need to be accentuated and multiplied. We collaborate not only with those on our current staff and in lay leadership; we also collaborate with those who have served before us, building on their work to reach even more people. One such example has been the monumental impact that English classes have played in opening doors to our international community. First Baptist Duluth had been offering English classes for many years prior to my arrival in 2010. These classes were well-attended and appreciated by the students and volunteer faculty alike. With an expanding vision for reaching international residents of our community, utilizing our English classes as a key element of outreach was an easy decision. One Voice Ministry Director SeungHee Rhe doubled the amount of class offerings by adding daytime classes to the preexisting nighttime offerings. ESL Volunteer Director Joy Goodman started a "reading club" with weekly readings from Scripture followed by question-and-answer sessions. It is a great joy to visit these classes and observe Muslims, Hindus, and Buddhists asking thought-provoking questions about biblical truths. Some of these classes have transformed into intentional discipleship groups. There are groups currently meeting that are comprised of a mentor with new believers, seekers, and doubters all interacting with the gospel message.

Chip Sweney, director of community transformation for Perimeter Church, a megachurch in nearby John's Creek, Georgia, has a profound appreciation for the work of First Baptist Duluth. He says, "It is a miracle that a 95-percent White Southern Baptist Church has developed an understanding of their multicultural community and devised a strategy to reach their changing neighborhoods." Chip's passion for developing a "theology of place," led him to begin *Unite,* a cross-cultural interdenominational community-focused movement of church leaders and nonprofit workers. In 2011, Chip published a book chronicling how this movement spread throughout the entire metro Atlanta area. In *A New Kind of Big: How Churches of Any Size Can Partner to Transform Communities,* he explains that the movement increases communication about larger community needs and provides a way to share workable strategies for addressing those needs. In the process, relationships form between leaders of diverse backgrounds, furthering the opportunity for holistic reconciliation within the church and community. Chip's closest friend in the movement is an African American pastor who calls him his "twin brother from another mother of a different color." Over the past decade, their friendship has allowed Chip a closer, more personal look at cultural inequalities that need to be addressed. He says, "Many church leaders don't have a clue. It's all about relationships. Until you get out and start talking to people and leaders and residents and going to local events, you won't really know your community."

The American church must attempt to escape from the
"me" mentality. Thomas Hammond warns churches: "You aren't
going to grow until you put into practice the things that you
have been taught." A healthy church will stretch people beyond
their comfort zone and into fields of needed service. Hammond
admits that Baptist churches and denominational structures are
currently being "stretched" into new areas and to greater capacity. "Probably half of the churches we plant in the future will be
non-Anglo. By the year 2050, Latinos will be the dominant cultural group in Georgia. We will be making a colossal mistake if
we do not prepare our structures to match the future paradigm.
This includes collaborating not only with church staff members,
but also expanding the reach of the church by connecting and
collaborating with leaders and institutions in the surrounding
community."

Duluth Mayor Nancy Harris says when she sees First Baptist
Duluth volunteers manning the concession stands at the high
school football games, she proudly says, "That's my church." Our
involvement allows parents of players to enjoy the game and not
worry about raising funds for their hometown team. This single
act of service has created tremendous goodwill in the community.
Pastor Abioye Tela works with local leaders to plan events in
the area, naturally creating a bridge from the community to our
church. First Baptist Duluth has served the community at holiday
events like Cookies with Santa or the community Easter Egg
Hunt. Our church has also served at summer celebrations on the
town's park lawn, and even more serious matters like passing out
water and facemasks during a racial equality demonstration in the
town center. When the city needs us, we are there!

Step Nine: Education

I have a master's degree in evangelism and a doctorate in church growth. I have taught evangelism on the undergraduate level at two institutions. Therefore, I am intimately aware of the homogeneous principle, the concept that people are most likely to be reached by someone who crosses the least barriers of difference. *Unite* leader Chip Sweney asks: "Is that the biblical model? I think not! Leaders must catch a vision. When people walk into your church building for the first time, do they see anyone who looks like them? First impression is everything." The homogeneous principle is a great evangelism tool, but cannot be used as an excuse for segregated worship services. People of color want to know: "Is there a place for me here?"

When the apostle Peter gave his sermon on the Day of Pentecost, he began his message with the phrase, "let me explain this to you" (Acts 2:14 NIV). In the confusion and chaos surrounding the fact that everyone was now hearing the message in their native language, Peter prioritized the need for everyone to understand what was happening in their midst. Attention was not drawn to the miracle, but rather to the magnitude of the message. Likewise, I do not want to use this book to merely draw attention to the diversity of my congregation. I wish to educate and challenge church leaders everywhere to seek ways to become culturally competent and understand what is happening around your church. Jesus said, "From everyone who has been given much, much will be required" (Luke 12:48 NIV). God has richly blessed our ministry; therefore, we are compelled, even obligated, to share our experience with anyone who would benefit from it.

My journey into multicultural ministry has provided the opportunity to meet a variety of denominational leaders. One such person is Neal Eller, whose ministry with Indian students you read about in chapter 7. As a nineteen-year veteran consultant for the North Carolina Baptist Convention, Neal describes our meeting as nothing less than a "God thing." After completing my previous book, *Technicolor: Inspiring Your Church to Embrace Multicultural Ministry*, Neal and his wife, Cherri, planned a visit to see First Baptist Duluth with their own eyes while visiting Atlanta on denominational business. Neal expressed that their original intent was to slide into the service incognito without any fanfare or intended meeting time. However, the Ellers came to our post-service meet and greet. Neal invited my wife, Glenda, and me to join them for lunch. That lunch meeting lasted about three hours. Neal and Cherri are similar in age to me, and immediately, I witnessed their excitement and interest in what had transpired at First Baptist Duluth. I also noticed their frustration in their inability to see this happen in other diverse population areas with similar prospects. Neal lamented that, as a convention leader, he often dreaded approaching pastors of our age because they seldom were willing to think outside the box and follow the leadership of the Holy Spirit to address their transitioning communities. This wonderful couple is living a multicultural life, opening their home to international college students and investing in their lives. God knit our hearts together very quickly. Soon, Neal invited our entire staff team to come to North Carolina and offered a two-day training seminar on strengthening the church through multicultural ministry.

Many churches are looking for a "starting point" to begin multicultural ministry. Perhaps the best place to begin is accessing the church's need to enhance cultural competence. Neal Eller has led his ministry team in a video-driven course titled "Cultural Mastery" by Ricardo Gonzalez. Eller laments that most churches are so far behind the demographic shifts in their community that they have no idea how to catch up. However, as Neal's diverse team of denominational servants has intentionally addressed cultural awareness, they have seen tremendous shifts in their interpersonal interactions, valuing one another more deeply and approaching one another in ways that increase cultural understanding.

Slowly, our church has seen the dream of Jesus' all-inclusive Great Commission become a priority in our everyday ministries and relationships. And we've had the great privilege to encourage and educate other churches in connecting with their increasingly diverse communities. Still, there is more to do. There are more to be reached and welcomed into community and fellowship. On Martin Luther King weekend, January 14, 2018, I shared with the congregation my dream as the pastor of this 135-year-old church in one of the most diverse counties in the nation:

I have a dream that one day . . .

Nigerians will worship alongside people from New York

Haitians will worship alongside people from Hawaii

Indians will worship alongside people from Illinois

Italians will worship alongside people from Indiana

And people from the Ivory Coast will worship alongside people from Iowa.

I have a dream that one day . . .

Peruvians will worship alongside people from Pennsylvania

Koreans will worship alongside people from Kansas

People from St. Kitts will worship alongside people from South Carolina

Venezuelans will worship alongside people from Virginia

Vietnamese will worship alongside people from West Virginia and Wisconsin

Jamaicans will worship alongside people from Jersey.

I have a dream that one day . . .

Afghans will worship alongside people from Alabama

Argentines will worship alongside people from Arkansas

Cameroons and Chinese will worship alongside people from Colorado

Canadians and Cubans will worship alongside people from Connecticut

Columbians will worship alongside people from California

Ecuadorians and Egyptians will worship alongside people from Florida.

I have a dream that one day . . .

Lebanese, Liberians, and Lithuanians will worship alongside people from Louisiana

People from El Salvador and Ethiopia will worship alongside people from Nevada

Bohemians will worship alongside people from Ohio

People from Benin and Brazil will worship alongside people from Oklahoma and Oregon

People from the Dominican Republic will worship alongside people from Delaware.

I have a dream that one day . . .

Mexicans will worship alongside people from Mississippi

Moldovans will worship alongside people from Michigan

Malawians will worship alongside people from Maryland

Russians will worship alongside people from Rhode Island

Tanzanians will worship alongside people from Texas

Thai and Taiwanese will worship alongside people from Tennessee.

I have a dream that one day . . .

Ugandans will worship alongside people from Utah

And people from Ghana, Great Britain, Guatemala, and
Guyana will worship alongside people from Georgia!

I have a dream . . .

The wonderful thing is that this is an increasingly accurate
picture of our congregation! After more than a decade of following the cross-cultural call of the Great Commission, I am so very
grateful to be living this dream today. I pray that God will give
you and your church a big dream, and that you will walk forward
confidently, knowing, "I am able to do all things through him
who strengthens me" (Phil. 4:13).

▼ ▼ ▼

Be Opened

by Darcy Wiley, cowriter

For years, Austin Chapman, who had been deaf from birth, could feel the bellow of bass notes and the beat of a drum as he watched friends dance to the vibration. Yet he had never heard the intricacies of a guitar part or the full range of a singer's voice. Music was an unreachable mystery to him. When he received a revolutionary new hearing aid at age twenty-three, it changed everything. Soon, his friends convinced him to post his news on Reddit. Responses flooded in with more than thirteen thousand commenters asking questions and listing suggestions for what songs Austin should be adding to his playlist as his device provided him a new level of hearing ability. One commenter suggested he start with classical genres and move forward through the historical progression of music. Another suggested, "'Clair de Lune.' It's like drops of silver honey drizzling over your eardrums." As the final song of Mozart's life, "Lacrimosa," played over the speakers in the car, Austin began to weep at the sound.

He said, "My old hearing aids were giving me a distorted version of music. They were not capable of distributing higher frequencies with clarity. Instead, it was just garbled gibberish." Austin had been perceiving only the deep, lower register of sound when there was an entire orchestra with layers of instrumentation waiting to be heard. With his increased ability to hear, Austin said, he finally understood the power of music. His friends wiped tears from their eyes, too, as they witnessed Austin enjoying music in a whole new way.[15]

Like Austin's years with his old hearing aid, many believers in Jesus remain limited in their spiritual hearing, settling for unclear and even distorted input that keeps them from feeling the power of the Spirit in their faith and ministry. If we will only let Him work, God is ready to lead us into a new level of clarity, growing our personal faith and our congregations' reach.

In one of Jesus' cross-cultural encounters in the Gospel of Mark, a group of friends in a Gentile region begged Jesus to lay His hands on a deaf man with speech impediments. The man could not understand or even hear the words that were being spoken about him. He could not ask a question or express his feeling of desperation. He could only feel the hands on his back as his neighbors nudged him toward this unusual visitor. Jesus was no showman, so He led the man away from the crowd to a place of stillness, giving His undivided attention to the man and his need.

Jesus began to examine the man, preparing him for the miracle that was about to take place. Rather than lay hands on the man as the community had begged, Jesus chose a very different approach. He placed His fingers into the man's ear canals, possibly communicating by touch the condition that He was preparing to heal. Jesus continued to probe without using verbal communication. He spit and then placed His fingers on the man's tongue. Scholars say that saliva was thought to have healing properties in Jesus' time, so seeing Jesus spit could have communicated to the man that Jesus was in the process of healing him.

I wonder how each of us might respond to this unconventional approach to our well-being. Maybe some of us would back away from Jesus, wanting more personal space, content to remain in our dull yet familiar state, untouched and unhealed. When it comes to our spiritual hearing, some of us may prefer that He leave our ears just as they are. Maybe through this book, Jesus is using His finger to examine and point out the closed places in you and your congregation. Maybe He is entering your personal space and communicating the transformation He wants to perform first in you and then in your church.

In my young adulthood, before Pastor Mark Hearn's move to Duluth, Georgia, he and I both served on staff at our church in Indianapolis. In that predominantly White congregation, we also had members from the Black community, a few Spanish-speaking friends, a Bangladeshi family, and an Iranian family. I see now that through that fellowship, God was priming Pastor Mark for what he would find in the even more diverse climate of Gwinnett County, Georgia. As I interviewed leaders from various backgrounds at First Baptist Duluth, I marveled at how God was working in similar ways in their individual lives, giving each of them a longing for multicultural fellowship and then directing their paths to bring them all together to serve in one place. As leaders and members have listened closely to the timeless call of Jesus and the current demographics of the community, they've helped their congregation return to the fullness of God's original design for the church.

As the members of this church have realized, when a monocultural church shifts to a wholehearted inclusion of all people, what appears to be a changing church is actually a church realigning with the DNA of the historical, worldwide church that Jesus initiated. In Isaiah 49:6 (NASB), as God is speaking to Israel, "He says, 'It is too small a thing that You should be My Servant to raise up the tribes of Jacob and to restore the protected ones of Israel; I will also make You a light of the nations so that My salvation may reach to the end of the earth.'" Those of us not from Jewish backgrounds were once the outsiders whom the early believers were called to reach. Now, we are adopted into that same calling. But hearing the invitation to live out this biblical, global gospel requires an unstopping of the spiritual ears, a return to full receptivity to Scripture and the Spirit, all senses and capacities opening to God's plan for us and the world.

When I first began the interviews for this book, I assumed that most longtime members from White backgrounds were hesitant about the demographic changes and the call that the leadership had presented to intentionally include the international community in the life of the church. What I found as I sat down across the table or screen-to-screen with these members was a hint of past hesitation among some, but also a rich legacy of crosscultural friendship and advocacy that prepared existing members for the changes that needed to take place in their church. Those who weren't won over by the need or by the biblical precedent for this type of ministry were eventually convinced as their peers in this increasingly diverse congregation lived out the all-too-rare reality of "They will know we are Christians by our love."

Before my full day of interviews on my weekend in Duluth, I took a walk through the empty church building. I noticed large photos from cultural celebrations like the Korean fan dance, a world map where members and visitors had marked their country of birth with a colorful magnet, and, of course, the brightly colored flags evenly spaced on the lower level and balcony representing attendees from more than forty-five nations. In true representation of Christ's love for the whole world, no single flag was placed in a more prominent position than another. As I walked along one wall, I stopped to read the inscription under a framed African cloth given to the church by a Ugandan couple: "*Upendo wa mungu umetuweka pamoja*," Swahili for, "The love of God has put us together." What I see happening at the church is a deepening and widening of vibrant, selfless love that seems to happen only in gatherings of diverse people of faith. When we segregate ourselves, we limit our personal growth and our gospel work. We shut ourselves off from the full hearing and expression of God's vast goodness. We shut ourselves off from one of the best pictures of heaven that we have here on this Earth.

On Sunday morning during my visit to First Baptist Duluth, the building began to buzz with conversation. Greeters poured coffee for those entering the building. A volunteer handed out church information printed in Korean, Vietnamese, Chinese, Spanish, and Portuguese. An interpreter distributed headsets in particular languages to those with limited English proficiency. A pair of friends from India and the state of Georgia sat together chatting in a pew. On the platform, worship leaders originally from Mexico, Korea, the Black community, and the White community stood side by side with microphones in their hands.

Together, we sang a song of gratitude, "Thank you. *Ganxie ni. Gracias. Gam-sa-hae*," switching easily between English, Mandarin, Spanish, and Korean. The most memorable part of the service came when we sang a call-and-response song with lyrics that hail from Revelation 5, one of the most worshipful passages in Scripture. Revelation 5:9–10 (ESV) says: "And they sang a new song, saying, 'Worthy are you to take the scroll and to open its seals, for you were slain, and by your blood you ransomed people for God from every tribe and language and people and nation, and you have made them a kingdom and priests to our God, and they shall reign on the earth.'" The most glorious worship is comprised of the words and melodies resounding from a unified group of believers from every background. What a powerful experience it was to sing of Jesus' worthiness and our shared identity as His people with a woman from India to my right and a woman from Nigeria to my left.

In recent years, I've become increasingly concerned about the health of the American church, as too many believers from White backgrounds have been content to remain in monocultural Christian circles. Some congregations have relegated their love for all the nations to faraway efforts, fearing the nearness of the people they would pay missionaries to go and serve. In this fear, many have celebrated ideologies that clash with the way of Jesus. I admit that I have sometimes wondered if their stubbornness is stronger than the influence of the Holy Spirit. I have wondered if my prayers for the softening of their hearts are sometimes lifted in vain. And in that process, I have become aware of the need to pray for my own spiritual hearing, that I would not, in my disillusionment, become closed off in my own way.

In one interview, I shared some of these thoughts with Kim Robinson, vice president for the North American Mission Board, who has, as a Black man, been on the receiving end of cultural exclusion too many times to count. In his comforting but challenging way, he told me, "We have to resist the temptation to believe the lie that a heart can't change. It can. Some people may die with a heart of stone, but we know the power of the gospel can change people, even through all kinds of difficulties."

Working on this book with Pastor Mark Hearn and spending time with his church members has made that truth clearer than ever. Through this church's transformation, I've seen that people can change with the consistent sharing of gospel truth and love, even if they seem set in their ways. Listening and helping tell the stories of legacy members and the newcomers they've eventually embraced has kept me tenderhearted and hopeful. This has been a faith-building work. I hope these stories build your faith as well, readying you to participate in the miraculous movement of God in your community.

Scripture tells us that in Jesus' interaction with the deaf man, after pointing out the areas of need, Jesus looked toward heaven, drawing attention to the source of the imminent miracle. He then breathed a deep sigh, empathizing with the man's suffering up to that point in his life while simultaneously revealing an intense longing for the day when He Himself would heal the world in its entirety. Jesus felt deeply. I imagine it showed on His face. After sighing, Jesus spoke aloud a powerful word in His language, "*Ephphatha!*—Be opened!" With that declaration, the silence of the man's ears opened up to sound. He could hear clearly. His mouth opened up to words. He could speak plainly. And as he spoke of the transformation he had found in Jesus, the reverberations echoed through the community. "They were completely amazed and said again and again, 'Everything he does is wonderful. He even makes the deaf to hear and gives speech to those who cannot speak'" (Mark 7:37 NLT). This is the kind of reaction I've heard time and time again as people witness the work God has been doing in the multicultural church. God makes it so that legacy members hear the call to diversity and find joy in it. He makes it so that language members hear in their own language, speak in a new language, and serve in their own special gifting and capacity. He makes it so that leaders leave behind mere human ambition and strategy and walk forward in Spirit-led ministry that reaches all people. Everything He does is wonderful!

We are living in a time of deep cultural shifts. Demographers say that the population changes we are seeing in metro Atlanta are going to be the reality for many areas in our nation in the next thirty years. As the full spectrum of culture becomes the norm at neighborhood groceries, schools, and playgrounds, shouldn't it be the norm in our churches, too? This could change everything, and that's not a bad thing. It's time for us to stop thinking about these changes as a problem and, instead, open our spiritual ears to the cultural diversity the church is meant to experience and encourage. As you have read about the mindset shifts in this particular church, I pray you sense the miracle that has occurred here and that you'll allow Jesus to come close and do another work of wonder in the neighborhood where you live and lead.

Hearing in Technicolor
Interviews

Abioye Tela, interview with Darcy Wiley (Zoom, January 2020).

Billy Chidester, interview with Darcy Wiley (Zoom, June 2020).

Cecil Nash, interviews with Darcy Wiley (Duluth, Georgia, October 2019 and Zoom, December 2019).

Charles Summerour, interview with Darcy Wiley (Zoom, November 2019).

Charlotte Kumar, interview with Darcy Wiley (Zoom, January 2020).

Chip Sweney, interview with Darcy Wiley (Zoom, June 2020).

Danny McCain, interview with Darcy Wiley (Duluth, Georgia, October 2019).

David Baba, email interview (September 2020).

Gilbert and Lucy Hong, email interview (September 2020).

Halimeh Ibrahim, interview with Darcy Wiley (Duluth, Georgia, October 2019).

Hugh Townsend, interview with Darcy Wiley (Zoom, June 2020).

Jeffrey and Anna Go, interview with Darcy Wiley (Duluth, Georgia, October 2019).

Joseph and Youngmi Kim, email interview with translation by SeungHee Rhe (September 2020).

Keith Murdock, interview with Darcy Wiley (Zoom, January 2020).

Kim Robinson, interview with Darcy Wiley (Zoom, June 2020).

KJ and SoYoung Lee, interview with Darcy Wiley (Duluth, Georgia, October 2019).

Leland Strange, interview with Darcy Wiley (Zoom, December 2019).

Letty Reeves, interview with Darcy Wiley (Duluth, Georgia, October 2019).

Li (pseudonym), email interview (September 2020).

Lindsay Lapole, interview with Darcy Wiley (Zoom, November 2019).

Mae (pseudonym), email interview (September 2020).

Mark Barneycastle, interview with Darcy Wiley (Zoom, January 2020).

Mayor Nancy Harris, interview with Darcy Wiley (Duluth, Georgia, October 2019).

Neal Eller, interview with Darcy Wiley (Zoom, June 2020).

Paola Villegas, interview with Darcy Wiley (Duluth, Georgia, October 2019).

Ray Lee, telephone interview with Mark Hearn (October 2020).

Steve and Julie Higgins, interview with Darcy Wiley (Duluth, Georgia, October 2019).

Thomas Hammond, interview with Darcy Wiley (Zoom, June 2020).

Tito Ruiz, interview with Darcy Wiley (Zoom, June 2020).

Todd Jones, interview with Darcy Wiley (Zoom, January 2020).

Tom Jones, interview with Darcy Wiley (Zoom, December 2019).

Victoria Ajayi, email interview (September 2020).

Virginia Jones, interview with Darcy Wiley (Zoom, October 2019).

Wilbur Brooks, interview with Darcy Wiley (Zoom, December 2019).

Notes

1. Alexandra Hasenpflug, "Hearing in Technicolor," YouTube TED Talk (August 4, 2016), https://www.youtube.com/watch?v=iGPLXHIopyc.

2. Annie Dickinson, "Seeing Sound: How Synesthesia Can Change Our Thinking," YouTube TED Talk (August 15, 2017), https://www.youtube.com/watch?v=88s6guf9egs.

3. William H. Frey, *Diversity Explosion: How New Racial Demographics Are Remaking America* (Washington, DC: Brookings Institution Press, 2015).

4. Jeffrey Passel and D'vera Cohn, "U.S. Population Projections: 2005–2050," Pew Research Center.

5. Thom S. Rainer, "Hope for Dying Churches," *Facts and Trends*, January 16, 2018.

6. Alan Deutschman, "Change or Die," *Fast Company Magazine*, May 1, 2005.

7. Scott Mautz, "Science Says This Is Why You Fear Change (and What to Do about It)," Inc.com, November 16, 2017, https://www.inc.com/scott-mautz/science-says-this-is-why-you-fear-change-and-what-to-do-about-it.html, accessed March 2, 2020.

8. Christopher Bergland, "5 Science-Based Ways to Break the Cycle of Rage Attacks," *Psychology Today*, December 2, 2016, https://www.psychologytoday.com/us/blog/the-athletes

-way/201612/5-science-based-ways-break-the-cycle-rage-attacks?amp, accessed March 2, 2020.

9. "Mere Exposure Effect," Psychology iResearchnet.com, https://psychology.iresearchnet.com/social-psychology/social -influence/mere-exposure-effect/, accessed March 2, 2020.

10. Korie L. Edwards, Brad Christerson, and Michael O. Emerson, "Race, Religious Organizations, and Integration," *Annual Review of Sociology* vol. 39 (2013): 211–28.

11. Stuart and Jill Briscoe, *Improving with Age: God's Plan for Getting Older and Better* (United Kingdom: CLC Publications, 2015), chapter 1.

12. Lisa Green, "Americans Believe Church Is Good but Dying," Lifeway Research, March 30, 2015.

13. Lifeway Research, "Churches Twice as Likely to Fear Refugees as to Help Them," February 29, 2016.

14. Adina Solomon, "Duluth's Demographic Destiny Train," Longform with Curbed.com, November 13, 2019, https://www. curbed.com/2019/11/13/20952131/gwinnett-county-duluth-atlanta -suburbs-demographics, accessed April 14, 2020.

15. Austin Chapman and Reddit Users, "I can hear music for the first time ever, what should I listen to?" Reddit.com user post updated 2012, https://www.reddit.com/r/AskReddit/comments/ xufi3/i_can_hear_music_for_the_first_time_ever_what/, accessed September 2020.